THE MAN BEHIND THE MILL

The Life and Stories of L. J. Maasdam

Constance S. Kramer

Copyright © 1996 by Constance S. Kramer

All rights reserved. Except as permitted under the United States Copyright Act, no part of this publication may be reproduced or distributed in any form or by any means, or stored in a database or retrieval system, without prior written permission of the author.

Contact Information:
The Maasdam Sorghum Mill continues to produce sorghum each year. For product buying information, to receive information about guided tours of the mill (fall only), to order more copies of this book, or to contact L.J. Maasdam or the author, write or phone:

>   Maasdam Sorghum Mill
>   6495 East 132nd Street
>   Lynnville, IA 50153
>   1-515-594-4369

Printed in the United States of America.
Library of Congress Catalog Card Number: 96-094123
ISBN 0-9643179-0-7

For Scott,

my husband and faithful encourager,

who introduced me to his grandfather,

Leonard J. Maasdam.

Contents

Pictures — vii

Maasdam Chronology — ix

Preface — xi

1 A New Sorghum Mill — 1

2 Cooking Sorghum: The Miraculous Cure — 13

3 The Great Depression — 17

4 Leonard Meets Gertrude — 25

5 Farmin' — 37

6 Hired Help — 47

7 In the Family Way — 61

8 Moving the Mill — 71

9 Mill Improvements — 83

10 Double or Nothing	93
11 The Digging Machine	105
12 Junkyards and Axles	123
13 Water and Wells	139
14 Two Round Houses	153
15 Sorghum Producers Organize	163
Index	171

Pictures

1.1 Leonard, Henry, Marie and Fred, 1916. .   9

4.1 Wedding portrait, 1934.   32

6.1 Ice cream at the sorghum mill, 1947. . .   57

8.1 Family at ten years, 1944.   73
8.2 Pans of boiling sorghum, 1950.   80

9.1 Leonard's "new" sorghum mill, 1947. . .   85

11.1 Leonard's POW-R-DITCHER, 1952. . .   106

12.1 Family at 25 years, 1959.   135

13.1 Leonard's irrigation system, 1957.   145
13.2 Maasdams in North Dakota, 1965. . . .   149

14.1 Leonard's first round house, 1973. . . .   155

15.1 Fiftieth wedding anniversary, 1984. . . .   167

Maasdam Chronology

1903	Lane Maasdam marries Henrietta Mathes (9/10)
1904	Leonard John Maasdam born (11/18)
1907	Henry Fred Maasdam born (9/30)
1910	Marie Elizabeth Maasdam born (11/6)
1912	Gertrude Susanna Wielard born (2/20)
1915	Fred Louis Maasdam born (11/25)
1925	Grandpa L. W. Maasdam dies (7/28)
	LJ contracts measles, bedridden fall and winter
1926	LJ meets Lola Jacobsen (summer)
	LJ starts making sorghum (fall)
1928	LJ contracts rheumatoid arthritis (spring)
	Lane injures foot in farming accident
1929	LJ begins 24 hour mill operation (until 1944)
1932	Marie marries Martin Vanden Hoek (12/22)
1933	Henry marries Cornelia Harthoorn (2/1)
	LJ meets Gertrude Wielard (May)
1934	LJ marries Gertrude (1/24)
	LJ starts farming for himself
	Grandpa Henry Mathes dies (5/10)
1936	LJ buys his first farm (March)
1937	Lawrence Willard Maasdam born (5/29)

1938	Fred marries Wilma Van Wyk (3/11)
	Darlene Joan Maasdam born (11/21)
1940	Marjorie Ellen Maasdam born (5/3)
	LJ's farm hit by tornado
1942	LJ begins moving the mill to his farm
1944	LJ begins to use steam to power the new mill
1949	LJ retires from farming
1951	LJ appears on *Double or Nothing* radio program
	LJ invents digging machine (winter)
1953	LJ breaks several ribs
1957	LJ and Gertrude move to Pella
	Lawrence marries Delores Jansen (2/14)
	Pella Irrigation Company founded
1958	Lane Maasdam dies (2/7)
	LJ takes flying lessons, earns instrument rating
1960	Marjorie marries Charles Kramer (2/19)
	Darlene marries Paul Schoon (6/4)
1965	LJ turns in silver certificates
1968	Henrietta Maasdam dies (8/31)
1972	LJ buys farm for development lots north of Pella
1973	LJ and Gertrude move into round house (fall)
1980	Sugar cane producers visit sorghum mill
1983	LJ begins *Sweet Sorghum Press* newsletter
1986	National Sweet Sorghum Producers and Processors Association formed (March)
1991	Gertrude Maasdam dies (1/23)

Preface

Someone once said, "A family is made up of what it remembers and what it forgets." So are individuals. The majority of the content for this book came from a series of interviews conducted with Leonard J. Maasdam on February 15–18, 1993. Most of the stories told come solely from his remarkable memory, although I have sought to verify them with family members and business associates. People's memories, no matter how good, tend to be rather selective. Some of the stories may seem to favor Mr. Maasdam, but that is the way he remembers them.

June 1995
Fort Collins, Colorado

Chapter 1
A New Sorghum Mill

Rural Lynnville, Iowa
Autumn 1926

Leonard John Maasdam let the screen door slam as he stepped out of the house and walked slowly across the farm yard toward the sorghum mill. The familiar smell of sweet sorghum cane cooking led him directly to the pan of boiling juice where, as expected, he found his mother Henrietta Maasdam nervously trying to manage the cooking while her brother-in-law Henry Van Wyk tried to show her one more time where she was supposed to be and what she was supposed to do. When she saw Leonard walking into the steamy room she said, "Len, what are you doing out here? You should stay in bed. You know them measles has got you so weak you can hardly walk!"

"Now Ma," Leonard replied, "You been in the house a dozen times already this mornin' and Uncle Hen needs somebody who's gonna stay in their place. I'm up and around now, so let me have those paddles!" He took them from her and began skimming the sticky green juice. The summer had truly been a rough one. When Leonard's dad had bought a cane mill last fall from the co-op in Kellogg, the whole family was excited to get it set up so they would get to make their own sorghum syrup for the first time in over fifteen years. Finally they would get to eat all the sorghum they wanted!

Leonard's father, Leendert, also known as Lane, was a tall, thin man. He was not a "typical" Maasdam because he tended to be more soft-hearted and trustful. He tried to get along with people and not give them a bad time.

Lane had made sorghum when Leonard was young, but quit after only two years. Leonard had always wondered if that was because of an incident his mother had once described. His father had hired a few men every year to work in the fields, and to cut the heads and strip the leaves off the cane. One time the workers were falling behind in getting the cane to the mill, so Lane, being a good-hearted man, hired another worker, only to learn later that winter that the boys had been loafing out in the field, and with the added man, had had even more fun. That incident humiliated him and he just quit making sorghum. Lane was somewhat involved with the new mill, but his heart was not in it the way it had been in 1910 and 1911.

Consequently, every year they had bought twenty-five gallons of sorghum from one of the neighbor families, either the Rozendaals or Van Gorps. They ate the sweet dark syrup three times a day on bread with

A New Sorghum Mill

their meals, and Henrietta cooked and baked with it too. Because they couldn't afford to buy more sorghum, by spring they always ran out and had to settle for corn syrup, which was not nearly as good.

Eating corn syrup instead of sorghum was almost as bad as having to eat baking powder biscuits instead of bread made with yeast. As he grew up Leonard remembered numerous times when they had to take biscuits in their lunches to school because his mother had forgotten to start the yeast the night before. One day he had his sorghum bucket dinner pail stuffed full of baking powder biscuits, and nothing else. He was so disgusted he brought the whole thing home and didn't eat any of it. When his father heard about it, he saw to it they had better meals for school.

Henrietta Maasdam was not a housekeeper. In fact, she hated anything to do with housework. She had not been trained how to cook and sew. As the oldest of two sisters, Henrietta helped her Dad outside with the milking and other chores. Her younger sister learned to work in the house. When Henrietta, a handsome young woman, got married at age eighteen she was not about to get stuck in the house. Even after she had children she would rather be out in the field hoeing cane than making dinner. Henrietta did not care much for fancy dressing, and in fact, disliked washing and ironing so much, that she and her children often looked unkempt. Sometimes Lane tried to make up for her deficiencies by ironing the children's clothes, but he had other responsibilities.

Leonard had started first grade in school before he

was even five years old because his teacher, who lived a half mile northeast, had come over and offered to give him a buggy ride to school every day, if he walked to the corner. His parents thought this was a good idea, so young Len, whose too-long brown hair fell across his eyes more often than not, went off to school. His parents had bought him a brand new pair of overalls for the year and he wore them proudly.

One day his teacher was a little late and the bigger boys had already arrived at school. When she drove up in the buggy, the boys grabbed the back of the buggy and pretended they were going to push it over. She took out the whip and hit them. They got mad, but didn't do that again.

One of Leonard's favorite recess activities in the winter was sledding down the huge hill in front of the school house. When the noon hour was almost over, the teacher opened the school door and rang the bell. As soon as Leonard and the other children saw the door open, but before she rang the bell, they hopped on their sleds and were a quarter mile away before the last notes died out. That did not go over well with the teacher either.

One day as Leonard was coasting downhill on his sled, he hit a bump and "upset the whole business." He cut his right index finger badly and never got stitches. The cut left a big lump and that was how he learned to tell his right and left hands apart. He just felt for the lump.

Most of Leonard's classmates were from French and English families and from the very beginning there was a distinction between them and the Dutch. There wasn't

A New Sorghum Mill

really friction, they were just two different cultures. The *Hollanders*, as they were known, were a different type of people. They were much devoted to church and religion; the *English*, as the people who were not Dutch were known, were not considered church-going people as much as the Dutch. The Dutch would not allow their children to play ball on Sunday or any other sports activities, whereas the English would let their children do anything they wanted, or so it seemed to young Len.

Leonard was talking to one of the English about eating at mealtime, and what they did if a piece of food dropped off the table. A Hollander picked it up and ate it, the English picked it up and threw it away. In general the Hollanders were more conservative and less wasteful. The English were more for spending and having a good time while the Dutch worked and saved and did not spend money so easily. Consequently, there was a division between the adults, and the children at school felt it too.

Although Pella had been founded as a Dutch settlement in 1847, the area around Sully had been settled much earlier by the French and English. Consequently, there were only a few Dutch families in the neighborhood. The Rozendaals, one of the Dutch families, lived one mile away from the Maasdams. At that time one country school was built every four square miles so no child ever had to walk more than two miles to school. Officially, the two families lived in different school districts, but since there were often not enough students for both schools to run, the schools were combined. Leonard appreciated the dozen children that the Rozendaal's had, because when they went to the same school, he had plenty of Dutch playmates.

They were at a disadvantage, however, because their families always spoke Dutch in the home and neither the Maasdam nor the Rozendaal children knew English very well. The children at school were determined to teach Leonard to "talk American." They took his cap and wouldn't give it back to him until he asked for it in English. Leonard wouldn't do it. He just repeated in Dutch over and over again, "*Geef mij mijn pet. Geef mij mijn pet.*" They wouldn't give it to him.

Leonard learned later that he had another disadvantage—he was hard of hearing—deaf to high-pitched sounds. Consequently, it was very difficult for him to learn, especially spelling, reading and music. Because he was a little different, and stuttered over his words instead of being a slick talker, he was one of the less popular kids and never learned to mix well with the other children. Sometimes they made fun of him.

When Leonard had an essay to write he used other methods. Since the teacher usually made them read their essays before the class, he took a blank paper to the front and read and read. That worked fine until one day the teacher decided to collect the papers after school. She and several classmates had even said it was his best yet! Another time he had to write an essay on, "What I like best." He wrote, "I like 'em both even up." It was short and easy. As always he came up with an answer he thought he could get by with.

Leonard was not like other kids. He did not like book learning in school, but if he could work with his hands

A New Sorghum Mill

he was much better off. When radio first started coming out, his parents didn't have the money to buy one. But Len wanted one very badly. He read everything he could about radios and one day saw an article in the newspaper, the first in a series showing how to build your own radio set at home! All he had to buy were coils, receivers and tubes. Of course Len couldn't afford much so he bought a vacuum tube for five dollars and a rheostat. He salvaged Model-T-Ford coils with the wires removed, and used oatmeal boxes for the base. He used an antenna from a Ford magneto, stretching it from the house to the barn. By borrowing the receiver from the telephone and the battery from the car he had a radio! The very first sound he ever heard on a radio was from WOI in Ames—on a set he built himself.

Because Leonard was different, he developed a sense for people that he used his whole life. He learned to watch people very carefully—perhaps because that was the only way he could understand what they were saying. He listened to their words, but also read their eyes and their facial expressions and began to discern much more than what they were saying. It soon became apparent to Leonard that God had given him the ability to *read* people's actions and react accordingly. His responses were sometimes a little bit odd—not exactly proper. Because he could set people on edge, he had the advantage.

Leonard remembered another lesson that he learned before he dropped out of school at the age of twelve, which stayed with him all of his life. That was the lesson about the Statue of Opportunity. The face of the statue was covered with long hair, the back of the head had short hair. The message that affected his life was this: when you see an opportunity coming (the long hair), grab it. If you wait too long the opportunity will be gone and you won't be able to reach anything (the short hair). He applied that lesson many times throughout his life—most of the time having to do with monetary advancement.

Leonard, as well as his brothers and sister often asked for various things that kids want. More often than not the answer was, "We don't have money in the bank for those things." Leonard was determined that when he grew up he would have money in the bank.

For instance, during a Fourth of July celebration when he was a boy, Leonard bought fireworks and told the neighborhood kids all about it. When they came over to see his display, he proceeded to charge them a small fee for the privilege of watching! One of his favorite tricks was to hang a stick of dynamite from a tree and blow it off. It exploded with an impressive BOOM and a big ball of fire. They heard the echoes from the explosion come back several times. He knew if he blew off the dynamite on the ground there could be danger from the flying rocks and dirt, but hanging in mid-air it was safe!

He also liked to demonstrate the homemade cannon he and his Dad had made. At first, Lane took a pipe and put some gun powder in it with a fuse to make a loud firecracker. But the pipe blew apart and there was danger of getting hit with bits of iron. At that time, the county tractor had broken an axle. The diameter of

A New Sorghum Mill

Figure 1.1: Leonard, Henry, Marie and Fred Maasdam, 1916. The two older boys had received brand new pens. Leonard was so proud of his, he didn't want to hide it in his pocket!

the shaft was big enough so that it wouldn't blow apart. They drilled a one-inch hole most of the way through the length of the shaft, and another hole in the side to insert the fuse. They put in some gun powder and lit the fuse. It worked! They put bolts in the tube and watched them fly ever so far!

Leonard had heard about a ship where sailors shot a rope from one ship to the other so passengers could get across. Since Leonard and his Dad were running out of bolts and had trouble finding them after they had flown so far, Leonard decided to tie a string to the bolt with a handkerchief attached. That way the bolts were easier to find. So the two put the bolt in the cannon and laid a fifty foot string neatly backwards. When the cannon went off the string broke cleanly—that's how fast the bolt was traveling. They tried it a few more times and then decided they needed to lay the string out in front of the cannon. As the bolt traveled, it gradually picked up the string, and took it, with the handkerchief waving, about a quarter of a mile. That was a pretty sight! And a loud noise too!

Leonard had been around dynamite ever since he was a little boy. When he was six, he and his three-year-old brother Henry, watched their Dad put some dynamite caps way up in the rafters in the buggy shed so they were out of reach of the children. The caps were the most dangerous part of the dynamite. The boys saw that box up there and figured out a way they could get it down. Their Dad saw them playing with the dynamite caps and asked them, "Now, how did you get those?"

The boys lied and said, "We just picked them up

off the ground." Lane was baffled. He was sure he had secured them better than that.

Leonard also loved to go fishing with dynamite. He threw a single stick into the river. The BANG killed the fish, who then floated to the top. He had one favorite spot on the river where one stick of dynamite brought a whole mess of fish.

These childhood experiences laid a foundation for the interesting man he would become.

Chapter 2

Cooking Sorghum: The Miraculous Cure

As a young man, Leonard was strong and healthy. He had dark hair, a long, thin face and an equally long, thin nose. Over six feet tall, he had broad shoulders and loved to work hard. During the fall corn harvest in 1925, Leonard picked an average of one hundred bushels of corn a day. One day he picked 139 bushels by hand. Few men could harvest that much because corn picking was such hard work.

Just after Lane bought the new sorghum mill in the fall of 1925, Leonard caught the measles. At that time, a vaccine for measles had not been developed, and having the measles could be a serious illness, sometimes resulting in retardation or inflammation of the brain. Leonard was sick all winter and by the spring and summer of 1926 was still hardly able to do any work. He would try to cultivate corn for half a day and then have to be in bed for three days. He didn't have the strength he used to have.

By fall, the Maasdam Sorghum Mill was really beginning to take shape, and Leonard was aching to be out there. He knew Uncle Hen needed him especially since his mother didn't know anything about making sorghum. He himself hadn't actually done much sorghum cooking, but from the time he had been a little boy he had watched his Dad on the farm. After his Dad quit making sorghum he had been over at the neighbors' mills watching them. He felt he pretty well understood the whole business. So, despite still feeling somewhat weak, he took hold of the paddles and began stirring and skimming the juice.

After only a few minutes in the steamy room he began to sweat profusely. The steam from the boiling juice was so thick that if he held his hand at arms length he couldn't see his fingers. And standing next to the pan, his greasy overalls got so hot that he couldn't even hold his hand on them. He was getting the best steam bath that central Iowa could offer and it was just what he needed to get the rest of the poison out of his system.

As Leonard's health improved, he tried to be out in the sorghum mill as much as he could. His Dad had built the furnace for their small operation and as Lane started cooking the juice, the skimmings kept boiling into the juice. Instead of separating out, they kept mixing in.

Leonard looked at the furnace and knew it was built wrong. He didn't know how he knew. Maybe it was from watching sorghum making at those other mills when he was a kid. More likely, it was his God-given talent to be able to see how things worked. Anyway, he just knew. His Dad had built it with brick all the way to the outside. With the fire underneath the whole pan there was no place for the skimmings to go so they just boiled into each other. Leonard told his father that the fire needed to be away from the front of the pan. Lane tore it down and built it the way Leonard said. It worked.

Perhaps next year they would plant more than ten acres of sorghum cane Leonard thought, *and make even more than a thousand gallons. And if they would just make a few improvements to the machinery he was sure they could get their yield higher than four to five gallons of sorghum per man per day.*

The family planted more cane and made more sorghum syrup the following year, almost three times as much. The year after that, however, in April of 1928, Leonard got sick again. This time he came down with a mysterious inflammatory rheumatism. For the first month he was in bed absolutely helpless. The swelling moved from one joint to the next with paralyzing pain. If he laid absolutely still, it wouldn't hurt, but he had to move sometime. His younger sister, Marie, tried to be his nurse. One day she helped him roll over for almost a half an hour. She finally took one of his arms and said, "Move!" For once *she* was telling *him* what to do instead of the other way around.

"I am moving!" he had crossly replied.

"No you ain't!"

"Get a microscope and you can see me moving!" He had always made a habit of putting things bluntly.

People generally knew where he stood.

The pain was intense, yet thinking back on the last weeks and months he couldn't understand it. While he hadn't been able to do any work and just lay in bed most of the day, it still had been one of the most contented times he could ever remember in his twenty-three years. The good Lord must have been with him, that was the only reason he could think of, why he had been so much at ease. It had been absolutely perfect.

Len's illness affected the whole family. In addition to nursing him, Marie had numerous other responsibilities. And Len's little brother, Fred, who had entered the seventh grade the previous fall, but had been held out of school for four weeks during sorghum making, was once again pulled out of school to do Leonard's farm chores. Since he missed so much school, Fred had to take the entire year over again.

Although Leonard was in bed for many months during those two years, he was constantly thinking about sorghum and what he wanted to do with the mill. It was so much a part of him, it was almost as if he had sorghum in his veins instead of blood.

Chapter 3

The Great Depression

By 1928 Lane and Leonard had located a larger mill in Missouri, and were on their way to making more and more sorghum with labor saving machinery. The two of them drove a one ton Model-T-Ford truck with hard rubber tires and a top speed of twenty miles per hour down south to look over the mill. They bought it and tore it down piece by piece, loading the lighter parts on the truck and shipping the rest by train. They didn't have any big machinery, so just rolled the mills up an incline and dragged the other parts over rollers.

The larger mill took more power to run, so Leonard had to find a twenty horsepower engine to replace the six horsepower one he had been using. He found one in good working condition on a farm sale north of Marshalltown for only five dollars.

With the stock market crash and the onset of the Great Depression, sorghum was in even greater demand.

Sugar was a luxury most families could not afford and so sorghum syrup became the main sweetener available. With it's high iron and potassium content, sorghum was a healthy and inexpensive substitute. Sorghum mills of varying sizes could be found every ten miles or so throughout the midwest. With corn selling at ten cents a bushel and hogs bringing in only two to three cents per pound, sorghum at sixty to ninety cents a gallon was a good money maker. As a result the Maasdam family never felt the hard times like other people did.

Just before the depression hit, in the summer of 1929, Leonard was driving on the highway one day and saw a big billboard with a picture of Uncle Sam on it and the words, "Nothing Can Stop the USA!". *Whoop*, he thought to himself, *why would they say something like that if everything was good? Hard times must be coming. We'd better be careful and not go into debt. We don't want to be in any risky financial positions.* He read the sign and saw through what the promoter was trying to say—that everything was okay. He figured everything *wasn't* okay or they wouldn't be trying so hard to convince him otherwise.

One of Leonard's favorite activities after the sorghum making season ended was to get in his Model-T-Ford touring car, drive through the countryside, and peddle sorghum house to house. He had a certain route that he traveled year after year and claimed that although he didn't have much formal schooling, meeting people and getting different ideas while out selling sorghum gave him the best education he could have had. Leonard didn't need to go to school to learn how to

The Great Depression

be a salesman. He used his God-given ability to watch the expressions and emotions that went across people's faces, and figured out what they were thinking and what they were going to do. He found that one of the best ways to sell sorghum was to get people to taste it.

One year they made a batch of sorghum that had soured slightly. It was nice looking but had an off flavor, so they didn't want to sell it to the grocery stores with their label on it. Leonard, not wanting it to go to waste, quickly volunteered, "I'll sell it door to door without the label on!" He loaded it in the car and drove off toward Grinnell. He made quite a sight. As always, he wore his denim overalls, showing little concern that they were torn, covered in oil spots, and sticky with sorghum. His filthy farm cap had a greasy thumbprint just under the bill where he took it on and off and he needed to shave. Irregardless, he stopped at one farm house, stepped out of the car and told the lady of the house, "I'm selling sorghum."

"Well," she asked, "is it any good?"

Not wanting to be dishonest, Leonard slyly suggested, "Listen, why don't you get a spoon, and I'll let you taste it!"

They went in the house and sat at the table. The woman tasted the sorghum and said, "My, that is good! I bought some last week at the store and I don't like it at all."

Leonard thought he knew what she might be saying and casually asked, "Do you have it handy?" Sure enough, it was some of their best sorghum with the label on. Before he left, the lady bought two gallons. *There's a lot of difference between being honest and being dishonest and still getting your way*, Leonard thought as he drove off the yard.

∞   ∞   ∞

Another time during the Depression years when Leonard was coming home from selling sorghum, a fellow stopped him on the road and asked him for directions to a place near Sully that had a stallion for breeding. Now, horses had become less and less popular as farming became mechanized during the late twenties and early thirties. But with the Depression, farmers could no longer afford machinery or the gasoline to run it. Seeing this man on the road made Leonard remember when he was five years old. He would go out with his granddad every Saturday morning to service their stallion. Maybe he should think about taking the opportunity to get into horse breeding. Maybe people would be buying horses again since they couldn't afford to buy equipment. They could raise their own "equipment" and only have to pay the stud fee and provide pasture.

It wasn't long before Leonard acted on his idea and bought a stallion. His Dad, Lane, couldn't do much work around the farm any more as a result of a foot accident, but was able to take the horse around for servicing at a ten to twenty dollar stud fee.

Lane Maasdam had had a bad accident earlier in the year. He and Leonard had been trying to install the new mill they had bought in Missouri. They poured concrete for the line shaft for the bearings that went to the engine. Then they decided to test the line shaft to see if they had put it in correctly by giving the big fly wheel a turn. But the concrete was too green and when the belt came off and lodged between the fly wheel and the pulley it jerked the line shaft off of the concrete foundation and threw a big chunk of concrete on Lane's ankle. His foot was left hanging on by the flesh with the ball joint sticking out at a right angle. He was in the hospital more than six months because the doctor was determined to save his foot. The ankle would have healed more quickly if they had amputated it. He wasn't able to do any work for a year or two. He walked with crutches first and later a cane, but he was determined to be able to help on the farm.

Sure enough horses did come back. Before long, they had more business than they could handle, so started looking into the purchase of another stallion.

"Len," that's what Leonard's Dad always called him, "We're gettin' so much business we need another horse. Let's put an ad in the paper and see what we can come up with." A man in Ogden had a cheap horse for sale. They went and looked him over, decided he looked good and said they'd take him. Leonard asked him, "Do you have your veterinary permit to show he's certified for servicing in the state of Iowa?"

"Well I misplaced it, I'll have to get another one," he mumbled.

They took his word for it, loaded the horse on the trailer and drove back in to town to pay him. Leonard asked again, "Now, where's your permit?"

"Well, I'll send it to you."

"No!"

"Now Len," his kind father gently stated, trying to ease the situation, "He said he'd send it, so let's pay him."

"No sir!" Leonard said to himself, *I don't trust this guy and I'm not going to let Dad go easy on him.* Turning to his father, Leonard stubbornly said, "There's a horse. There's a truck. You take him home. I'm not riding home with you. Now, where's the vet's office?" Leonard spoke to his father that way other times. Sometime during Leonard's teen years, Lane had lost control of him. Leonard was extremely stubborn, but he was also smart. Because Lane wasn't as hard-headed and strong-willed as he was, Leonard didn't show respect for his father as he should. After Lane's accident, he wasn't able to make Leonard respect him physically either.

The man selling the horse lied and said, "I don't know. I don't have any use for one." The office was only a block away and so, like it or not, they all walked over and the local guy got a bawling out for trying to sell a horse that didn't pass the tests at all. Lane and Leonard kept looking.

They heard about another horse for sale in Fort Dodge. After his last experience, Leonard was expectedly cautious. Before going to see the horse, Leonard drove through the area selling sorghum, "happening" to stop at this man's neighbors. "Your neighbor has a fine horse!" he casually remarked hoping to find out about the man's reputation locally. He found out the man did indeed have fine horses and a good reputation. They were in business. Lane had a full-time job for three or four years. Finally in the late thirties, as prices improved, farmers went back to the convenient, time-saving tractor. Stud servicing was good while it lasted!

Chapter 4

Leonard Meets Gertrude

From the time that he dropped out of school in the eighth grade until he got married at the age of twenty-nine, Leonard had lived at home. As he looked back upon it, he didn't find it unusual that his father had never paid him a wage or given him a cut of the profits from the sorghum mill. He was one of the children and still living at home. They bought him what he needed and gave him a little money now and then to spend on other things.

Leonard never had the courage to date girls very much. He was too bashful. But when his second cousin Lola Jacobsen came to visit the farm all the way from northwest Iowa in the summer of 1926, he had a great time. She came with her parents and brother and sister. Despite still feeling weak from his bout with the measles the previous winter, on Saturday night Leonard decided to take Lola and her siblings, along with his brother and sister, Henry and Marie, to Pella for a band concert at church. Even though she was eighteen months older than he, Leonard and Lola hit it off right away. When she left for home four days later they decided to write letters back and forth. Leonard remembered how anxious he was to see her when they planned a trip to the Grotto in West Bend, or to Clear Lake for the Fourth of July.

One time he took her to the state fair. Even then, he was interested in airplanes so he asked, "Lola, do you want to go for an airplane ride?" Despite a few misgivings, Lola was a good sport and gave in. The airplane had an open cockpit so they both awkwardly climbed in.

After settling themselves into their seats, Lola was dismayed, "Look at all these oil spots on my dress! What am I going to do?" Climbing into the cockpit with the engine running had ruined her dress. The pilot of the plane overheard her cries and after the ride, gave them their money back. Leonard liked the free ride!

The two kept their long distance relationship intact for two years. At first, Leonard couldn't understood why she abruptly wrote him a letter ending the whole thing. What he painfully could understand was the rejection he felt when she quit dating him and married someone else. He had wanted to marry her so badly. Just after he received Lola's letter, in the winter of 1928, he drove all the way to Humboldt to talk to her in person. The trip didn't do any good—they both burned all the letters they had written—and five months later Lola wrote a letter to Henry, Leonard's brother, telling him she had married Jack Thorn.

Leonard was at church a few weeks later as usual, still thinking about the "Dear John" letter he had received. *Why had she done that?* He couldn't understand it. The service opened with the old hymn, "Have Thine Own Way Lord" and it's simple message comforted him as nothing else could.

> Have thine own way, Lord! Have thine own way!
> Thou art the potter; I am the clay.
> Mold me and make me after thy will,
> While I am waiting, yielded and still.

He prayed the prayer he had prayed many times before, *Lord please give me a life partner so that I can have a Christian home blessed with children.* But it wasn't until five more years had passed that he met the woman he would one day marry.

Many years later, thinking about his relationship with Lola, Leonard realized that he had never really talked about marriage while dating her. He simply assumed they would marry. What Lola saw, though, was a very weak and sickly young man. That was confirmed when only a few months after she wrote her letter, Leonard was once again bedridden—this time with a case of inflammatory rheumatism that lasted for weeks. Leonard decided that she had not seen any future in him. He would not let that happen again.

As a youngster, Leonard went to church with his parents every Sunday afternoon. They didn't have church in the morning because it was too hard to get the chores done on time when they had to ride in a buggy for an hour just to drive the four miles to town. Later, when they got a car it was much easier and then they went to Question School in the middle of the week too.

When Leonard was fifteen he felt led to join the church. He didn't really know why. He had faith in God and it was just something he felt he wanted do. He wanted to be honest and square with everyone in his life, even with his Maker.

Like young people have done for decades, Leonard and his buddy liked to drive around the square in Pella after church on Sunday nights. One such night in May, they noticed three girls sitting on a park bench, and stopped to talk to them. Leonard was amazed when they asked, "Can we go along with you?" Of course they had to have partners, so his buddy hopped out of the front seat and climbed into the back where one of the girls joined him. Gertrude Wielard got in and sat right next to Leonard. She was average in height and build, but had dark, naturally curly hair, and straight teeth in a pleasant smile. He thought she was a young, pretty girl. She looked swell! Her cousin Joseline sat next to the door. Pretty soon Leonard had dropped everyone off except Gertrude—then he had her to himself. He had two ways to take her home, the long way or the short way. He chose the extra one-to-two miles so he could spend a little more time with her.

They met in 1933 at the height of the Great Depression. Every Saturday night Leonard drove to Pella to pick up Gertrude. They drove around town and talked

Leonard Meets Gertrude 29

to other young people. Sometimes Gertrude's cousin Joseline came along. She was a real flirt.

Once the three of them were sitting on a park bench in the Square with Gertrude in the middle, and Leonard put his hand behind Gertrude's back to tickle Joseline. That made Gertrude angry and jealous. What Leonard didn't tell Gertrude was that he never had any interest in anyone but her. He was just teasing.

Quite often Leonard also drove to Pella on Sunday night. One weekend soon after they met, the Skunk River went out of it's banks so Leonard had to miss a date. They had telephones but Leonard never considered using a telephone for such a frivolous thing as a date cancellation. He hardly even remembered he had a telephone as his folks rarely used it. Because it didn't work very well over long distances anyway, they had to repeat a lot to be understood. Consequently, Gertrude wondered for a whole week whether he was coming back or not.

While Leonard was courting Gertrude, he showed himself to be a very generous beau. He brought her a Mr. Goodbar candybar every week! Each candybar cost five cents in the store, but Leonard had bought a full box wholesale, so his candybars only cost three cents each! He found out later Gertrude liked the foil the candybars were wrapped in better than the sweets themselves. She made pretty pictures with them.

When the two of them met, Leonard was driving an older Oldsmobile sedan. Within three months of meeting Gertrude he bought a brand new Chevrolet car, wanting to show her that he could amount to something.

Considering this was during the depression years, that was quite a feat. Gertrude was impressed, and she liked learning to drive it!

On the Fourth of July, Leonard and Gertrude took another couple in Leonard's new car and drove all the way to the Amana Colonies in eastern Iowa. They had a grand old time, especially Gertrude, since she had never been that far away from home before. Although they both had been satisfied with each other and progressed steadily in their relationship, it was that day, July 4, 1933, that they started getting more serious. They spent the whole day and the evening together and Leonard began to think that she was the answer to his prayers of so many years.

Since he met Gertrude at the Square in Pella, Leonard didn't know anything about her or her family. Although she had a Dutch name, she was a stranger to him. Leonard never wanted to get into anything unprepared so he decided to find out something about her. Gertrude's folks lived outside of Pella, so one day after a recent rain, Leonard drove out to meet her neighbors. The dirt road she lived on was muddy so he parked his new car and walked in. Soon he came to a house and saw a thirteen year old boy out front playing. "You live here?" he questioned.

"Who's askin'?" the boy answered.

"Johnny Green."

"Yeah, I live here."

"Who lives in that house down the road?"

"Them's the Wielards."

"Hmm, Wielards. I heard of them before. Don't

they have the two girls, Gertrude and Johanna?"

"Yep, that's them."

"What kind of girls are them girls?"

"Just normal average girls. They're nice enough. What you wantin' to know for?"

"Jest wonderin'."

Satisfied that she seemed like a sensible young girl that he could trust, Leonard worked his way through the mud to his car and continued his weekly dates throughout the fall and winter with Miss Gertrude Wielard. Their relationship gradually progressed until they both assumed an unwritten, unspoken, but mutual agreement that they would one day get married.

They talked in January about getting married in the spring. One night they were over at Gertrude's folks' house talking about the farm Leonard had already spoken for. They planned to live in Grandpa and Grandma Mathes' house across the garden from his folks after they got married. Leonard would farm his grandfather's 120 acres for four dollars cash rent per acre. As they were sitting at the kitchen table Leonard told Gertrude, "We'll live on love and kisses if you'll be my missus." Then he suddenly stood up, took Gertrude's hand and pulled her to her feet. Walking over to the calendar on the wall he said, "Which day do you want to get married?" They put a mark on the twenty-fourth of January and that was that. Neither of them wanted to wait until spring.

Considering the times, Leonard and Gertrude did not plan a fancy wedding. They were married in the afternoon at his Grandma Mathes' house in Sully with

Figure 4.1: Leonard and Gertrude Maasdam wedding portrait, January 24, 1934.

only the preacher and family members present. Gertrude wore one of her good dresses—the one with the drop waist, appliqued flowers on the sleeve, and an imitation carnation on the bodice. Leonard obligingly wore a dark suit coat, which, of course, was not new. Leonard didn't want to have an expensive reception after the wedding, so they ate with the family and then drove over to Gertrude's folks where they spent their first night together.

Leonard remembered how there were two bedrooms in the upstairs of her parent's house. When he got up there and went into the room that had been made up for them, Gertrude was nowhere to be seen. He sat there a while wondering where she was, until he heard the door open from the other bedroom. She had changed into her nightgown and was now ready to come to bed!

They left the next morning on their honeymoon and drove all the way to Lincoln, Nebraska to stay at Gertrude's relatives, the Rapp's. They stayed for two and a half weeks and, as Leonard later recalled, "Where else could we get free room and board? Jimminy Christmas, them was hard times!"

At that time when a couple was newly married, shivareeing was a common practice. A group of young people went over to the couple's house and peeped in on them until they were noticed. Then the couple invited the group in for treats. Sometimes the youngsters played pranks like putting a spring wagon on the roof, or practical jokes that got them into trouble.

One time Leonard went out with a group of boys to go shivareeing. He always had fun because he liked to hang around outside and watch the couple through the windows without their knowing they were being watched. Sometimes when the boys had seen enough and were ready to be invited inside for their treats they set a shotgun against a window sill and fired it. The noise and vibration from the windows shook the whole house and the couple knew they were being shivareed. On this particular night the boy with the shotgun had more "ambition than sense," as Leonard said later. The boy set the shotgun next to the window on the front porch. When he fired it, he blew a gaping hole in the roof!

Soon after they were married Leonard and Gertrude were having a reception with Gertrude's folks in their house south of Pella. Everyone was sitting in the kitchen and Leonard was in the doorway next to the hall by the stairs. *Now this is an old house*, he thought to himself, *but there sure seems to be more creaking tonight than usual.* "Did you hear that?" he asked his new mother-in-law. "I never heard this house creak like that before." But no one seemed bothered so Leonard decided he wouldn't make a commotion either. But it sounded like somebody was on the roof.

While their guests were enjoying the refreshments, one of Leonard's friends noticed their mark on the calendar for the twenty-fourth of January. "What's the matter Leonard, were you afraid you'd forget which day you was gonna marry her?" Everyone laughed and had a lot of fun with that.

They all went to bed and the next morning Gertrude's mother was all excited. "Dad," she exclaimed

Leonard Meets Gertrude

to her husband, "I can't get this stove to draw! Take the pipes out and see if anything is plugged!" Her husband patiently disconnected the pipe where it went into the stove. That looked clear. Next he took it out by the ceiling and peered down the pipe. Everything was open downstairs.

"Leonard! Gertrude!" he hollered upstairs where the newlyweds were still sleeping. "Come on down here. We need your help!" Somebody was getting a ladder, but to Leonard they seemed to be taking an awfully long time. Never one to waste an opportunity he hopped on some boxes stacked beside the house and was soon on the roof looking things over. He discovered the problem immediately. The pranksters had stuffed a gunny sack down the chimney! He pulled it out and whooof!, all the soot in the chimney was loosened and fell into the kitchen leaving a cloud in the air and a layer of dirty ash covering everything. Gertrude's mother was so angry she didn't even know what to say.

Leonard and Gertrude lived with her folks about a month after they were married and then lived with his folks until they were ready to move into Grandpa and Grandma Mathes' old house in March. They got shivareed again in that house, but they were expecting it that time and nothing mischievous happened.

Chapter 5

Farmin'

Leonard and Gertrude lived in Grandpa's home for three years and never paid a penny for house rent. They cash rented his 120 acres and planted them in corn, oats, hay and, of course, sweet sorghum cane. Lane had given them four horses, four milk cows, and six breeding sows when they got married. They milked the cows and sold the cream to buy groceries. Gertrude also raised chickens. She kept some for laying hens and sold the rest to the grocery store for broilers. Leonard's younger brother Fred, who was unmarried and still living at home, farmed their father's 140 acres.

Ever since Lane's foot accident in 1928, Leonard and his siblings could not get along. Once his father was no longer able to be boss of the farm, Leonard, as the oldest, lost no time in taking over. His father never said he was actually the one to be in charge, but he tried to be boss over Henry, Marie and Fred anyway. They wouldn't take it from him.

When it got to be fall, the Maasdam's had a lot of corn to pick. Henry said, "Well, I'm going to pick corn today."

"Oh no you ain't, Hank," Leonard responded, "You need to go out and sell sorghum. You load up twenty cases and bring them to Knoxville. We'll hire a bunch of boys and get all that corn picked after we get the sorghum sold. You don't have to start by yourself."

Henry didn't say a word. He hated it when Leonard called him Hank and Leonard knew it. He just walked to the barn, hitched a team of horses and went and picked a load of corn. Almost every morning Leonard pestered Henry to go out and sell sorghum. Henry would go to the barn, get his team ready and head for the corn field. He wouldn't listen to Leonard at all.

By 1933 Marie and Henry had both married and moved off the farm, leaving only Fred to butt heads with his brother. Leonard, being eleven years older than Fred, was the logical choice to be in charge of the farm. But Fred, like Henry and Marie, did not like taking orders from Leonard and resented working under him. The three siblings claimed that Leonard took the easy jobs like going to town to pay bills and buy things, while the rest of them had to work. There was some truth in their claims, because Leonard was still somewhat weak from his illnesses. It took years before he fully recovered his strength.

The year Leonard and Gertrude got married was a very dry year for farming. They had planted oats, clover, corn and cane. Early on, Leonard saw that their crops weren't going to amount to anything, but there was still time to disk them up and plant cane. Fred came over one morning just after they had had a little shower of rain so there was moisture in the ground. "What you hookin' up the disk for Leonard?" he questioned.

"I can see we ain't gonna get nothin' out of them oats or clover so I thought I'd take these horses out and plant me some cane."

"Well I'm gonna do it good!" Fred exclaimed. A little later he hooked up the plow and deeply furrowed his ground before planting the cane.

Leonard disked the field and planted the field, and it germinated and grew. Fred's did hardly anything. The plowing had turned the soil over too much and with the little bit of moisture gone, the seeds did not germinate. In the fall, Leonard had a crop of cane to put through the mill and Fred hardly had any, which made him angry. The two brothers just could not get along.

Although Leonard wanted to farm when he got married, 1934 was still the height of the Great Depression. He was always anxious to "do the right thing" (as long as it was his way), and knew that it wouldn't be wise to buy acres of ground for fear he might lose it all. So shortly before he married, Leonard invested two thousand dollars in some stock at ten dollars per share. The stock market had already crashed and the prices were low. Farm prices were low too, but he reasoned that since the stock market had dropped first, it would also come back first. Then when he sold the stocks he would have a little more money with which to buy land.

Sure enough, in a few short years he more than doubled his investment. In November of 1935, Leonard put in a bid of nineteen thousand dollars for the 240 acre farm just around the corner from where his folks lived. He put two thousand dollars down for a deposit. He didn't know about the necessity, however, of putting a time limit on his bid. Soon the land company came back saying they wanted three hundred dollars more than what he had offered. "Whoop," Leonard told him, "I ain't payin' that." So the land company sent an agent to his neighbor, who was always looking for the easy road, and offered to cash rent the farm to him if he'd do some work on the buildings and try to improve the place.

When Leonard found that out he stubbornly went to the land agent in Grinnell and demanded, "If you're going to rent the place to him, I want my money back!"

"Now Mr. Maasdam," the agent tried to soothe him, "let's see if we can't get this settled..." He talked very nicely, but didn't do anything. By the third of March, however, they had written Leonard a letter and he had the place. As it turned out, the incident with his neighbor was just a scam to get that extra three hundred dollars. Leonard had learned a valuable lesson: when you make an offer for land, make sure it has a time limit on it.

Leonard and Gertrude moved into the house on their new farm, and he farmed both places until 1938 when his younger brother Fred got married to Wilma Van Wyk and *they* wanted to live in Grandpa Mathes' house and farm his ground. That meant that the hired man who had been living there would have to move out. Just across the river there was a sixty-three acre farm for sale. Leonard went to the man who owned it and paid thirty-eight hundred dollars for the whole thing. Then they had a house for their hired man.

 A little later another farm across the river came up for sale and Leonard found out at a farm sale that the neighbor who was in cahoots with the land agent was interested in buying it. Leonard didn't even go home that night. He drove right through Sully and Lynnville and onto the yard where the owner lived. "I hear you have your farm for sale. Is that right?," Leonard asked, not wasting time for pleasantries.

 "Yeah," he said.

 "What are you askin' for it?"

 "Sixty dollars an acre."

 "Would you care to meet me at the bank tomorrow morning when it opens and I'll have a check made for you."

 "Shore will," he said.

 Leonard wasn't interested in getting more land, he just didn't want his neighbor to get it. A while later another neighbor sold him an additional sixty acres across the river for three thousand dollars. By now Leonard had plenty of ground and he kept his hired man busy. Ever since their father's accident with his foot, Lane was never able to work the same, so the family hired Floyd Vargas to work on the farm as a hired man.

 Floyd had been working on their farm for a number of years, and Leonard always thought he was kind of an oddball 'fella. He had a car and always went home for the weekends to his folks' place thirty miles to the east. One time he had gone to Newton for Saturday night shopping, to buy a pair of nine cent socks. Before the week was out he had holes in them already. So that weekend he drove all the way over to Newton to get his money back before he drove home.

In the summer they had to cultivate the corn—each one using a one row cultivator and a team of horses. "Flor," Leonard suggested, that's what he liked to call Floyd, "why don't you pick which cultivator you want to use, and then put it in order just the way you want it." He knew Floyd was the kind of guy to blame somebody else if something wasn't working. By giving him first choice and as much time as he wanted to fix it up, Leonard was laying a trap for him. Sure enough, they were cultivating a week later and Floyd was doing a lousy job.

"Well it ain't my fault, Leonard," he whined defensively. "You gave me the worst cultivator."

"Now listen, Flor...," and Leonard gave him the whole run down.

One thing Floyd did well was hoeing. For some reason he liked doing that better than cultivating. Leonard's mother did most of the hoeing, since all the cane needed to be hoed by hand, but Floyd was at it on this particular day. He hoed the tops of the weeds off and then Leonard followed him with the cultivator. They only had about twenty rods left, half of it on the hillside and half of it on the bottom. Leonard was anxious to finish up since it was the Fourth of July so he told Floyd, "Just hoe over here where its the weediest so we can hurry up and get this finished."

"If I can't hoe it all, I'll quit," he said.

"Just quit then!" Leonard retorted. "This is what I want you to do and no more." He walked back over to where he had been cultivating, clicked to the horses and glanced back over at Floyd. He was over in the wrong place again! Leonard stopped the horses and strode over to where he was hoeing. "I told you in no uncertain terms I did not want this part hoed," he yelled.

"Well then I quit."

Leonard lost his temper. "You see that crick there? You see the house up there? I want you to take the hoe, go across that crick, up that hill and go home!" With that Leonard turned around and stalked back to his cultivating. He glanced out of the corner of his eye and saw old Floyd hoeing right where he was supposed to. *Why he had to get that tough with the guy to get him to do what he wanted him to, he didn't know. But he knew if Floyd couldn't obey orders he didn't want him around.*

Fall harvest time on the farm was always busy, but even more so on the Maasdam place because they had to make sorghum too. So Leonard taught Floyd how to cook sorghum and Floyd did a good job of it. But he didn't want his overalls washed! He got them so sticky with sorghum that they got good and hard. He figured that way they wouldn't wear out so fast when he was picking corn!

Marie collected the washing on Saturday night, so after Floyd left for his folks, Marie went and picked up all his clothes (his overalls were stuck under the bed), and brought them to the wash house with the other laundry.

On Monday morning Floyd walked in and asked Marie, "Where's my overalls?"

"I want to wash them," Marie replied.

"Well I want to wear them, now where are they?"

Marie showed him, so he worked another week wearing them the way they were. The next Saturday he had hidden them even better. But Marie hunted until she found them and then went to the wash house and put them in a tub of water to soak. On Monday morning Floyd came in asking for his overalls again. "They're in the wash house," Marie told him smugly. Floyd went to look, and came back five minutes later.

"I can't find them, where are they?"

Marie innocently answered, "Did you look behind the door in the tub of water?"

Floyd had his ways, but in general he was a good sorghum cook. Except one day when he was cooking he got the pan out of order. The fire was down and putting heat on it was liable to make the pan boil over. Leonard questioned him, "Flor, why ain't you got any fire in there? You're supposed to be boss of the fire man to tell him whether you want more heat or not. Come with me and let's get this straightened out." They had a three by three foot railroad car on some tracks leading to the wood pile out back and Leonard told Floyd, "Load up some wood." Leonard took it over to the firebox and ordered Joe, the fire man, "Put it all in."

Floyd raised the roof, "What are you doing? I'm not gonna be responsible for boiling that pan over."

"No you ain't, because I'm doing it. Now go get another load of wood and put it in the fire." Floyd

Farmin'

raised the dickens, but did as he was told. "Now why don't you get one of them old car tires on the hill. They make a terrific heat." Leonard was enjoying himself, but old Vargas got so mad he finally walked out and sat on the hillside. He had threatened to walk out before but had never actually done it. So Leonard took over and got the pan back to normal, and then Floyd was ready to come in and cook some more.

Floyd Vargas wasn't the only hired hand around the Maasdam farm. Every winter Leonard hired men to go out in the timber and cut wood to fuel the furnace for sorghum making the next fall. Then in the fall he hired up to thirty additional people to help make the sorghum. They were paid one dollar a day, plus room and board. The family had the upstairs fixed so that ten men could sleep at a time. The women changed the sheets between the night shift and the day shift. The boys didn't go back and forth from home to work because it took too long. Since her mother wasn't interested in cooking meals, Marie and two other young women were responsible for preparing the food for the twenty or more hungry men three times a day for both shifts. After Leonard and Gertrude were married, Gertrude and her sister Johanna helped too. When the mill ran twenty-four hours a day, Henrietta Maasdam spent most nights down in the sorghum mill making sure the hired help weren't loafing.

Chapter 6

Hired Help

From 1929 to 1944, the sorghum mill had to run for twenty-four hours a day, six days a week. The crew usually tried to finish by midnight on Saturday night so they wouldn't have to work on Sunday. In the fall, there was only a short period of time after the sorghum cane matured, until the first killing frost. They had to get all of their acres harvested during this time.

 Harvesting the cane was a difficult task, especially in the early years when everything had to be done by hand. It took nearly half a day to get a load of cane ready to go through the mill. The boys first had to cut the ten to twelve foot stalks out of the field, chop the heads off and then strip the leaves off. Leonard usually hired boys who had just left the eighth grade and didn't plan to go on to high school. They used eight wagons with two horses pulling each one. In 1928 they bought a corn binder to cut and bundle the cane mechanically which speeded up the process.

The men in the field were responsible for keeping the pile of cane well supplied throughout the day and night. They couldn't be out in the field all night, but because the mill ran around the clock, towards late afternoon they piled the stack of cane tall enough to last until the next morning. On one particular day there wasn't nearly as big a pile as there normally was at that time. Although Leonard had taken charge of the sorghum operation, his father was still around. When Lane noticed that the cane pile was unusually low he suggested to Leonard, "Maybe we should send another guy to the field. It looks like we're short of cane. There won't be enough to run all night."

Leonard looked at the small size of the pile and immediately recalled the incident his mother had told him about years ago. The men should have had more cane piled up. Leonard thought, *whoop I'm not going to make that mistake.* Feeling the anger inside him, Leonard spouted, "I'm not gonna send another man out there. They've been loafin'! I'm gonna go out there and take one away!"

Lane nearly blew up, "What do you think you're doing, taking one away? The mill'l run out of cane before midnight!"

Leonard didn't even bother to argue with him. He just slammed the door as he got in his car. Lane walked away, shaking his head. Somehow he had not taught Leonard how to control his temper. Leonard drove out to the field. "You guys been loafin' all day," he yelled at the surprised workers, "I've got work for a spike loader back at the farm so I'm gonna take a man away. And I want to see that pile taller than yesterday's before quittin' time. Now get busy!"

When men were working hard and trying to do their best, Leonard respected them and gave them a lot more leeway. But when they were shirking and doing it so badly that he knew they were shirking, he could add it all up and let them have it. He knew the secret in that situation. He could say anything to them and get by with it. Leonard believed in an honest, hard day's work, and he knew how to get it.

Sure enough, before dark the mill had one of the biggest stacks ever piled outside waiting to be made into the sweet dark syrup. And all Lane Maasdam said was, "Well, I guess Len knows what to do."

Once the cane was harvested, it was brought to the sorghum mill in wagons. One man carried the bundles off the slanted wagon and threw them on the table. That was the hardest work. Another man pulled them straight, cut the string that held the bundle together, and then cut off the heads with a sickle. A third man fed the stalks evenly up a conveyer and through the mill where the juice was squeezed out, ready to cook. The men alternated jobs so no one had to work harder than another.

One time the boys were complaining to Leonard that Jacob, the one doing the feeding, wasn't doing it right. He let bundles get through whole and they continually plugged up the mill. Everything had to stop before they could squeeze any more cane.

Leonard told Jacob, "Now I don't want you back

by the mill. You can throw on the table once and pull heads twice."

"If I can't go all around, I'll quit," Jacob answered.

Leonard had thought the whole thing through and knew someone else he could hire. "Okay, you're fired. Just go."

Unprepared for such an answer Jacob sputtered, "Well, who you gonna get to run the mill?"

"That's none of your damn business," Leonard responded and that was it. With the hired help he consistently tried to call their bluff. He would not let them get the best of him. He tried to anticipate things enough ahead of time so that he never had to back up. And when it was time to crack down he tried to do it right. He tried to apply the short little phrase his father had taught him, "Be sure you're right," to his hired help, his business, and his own personal life. Leonard was determined and overbearing, but he had his reasons. He knew what he wanted and that was it.

Leonard had trouble with another 'fella, Marvin, that same year who thought the work was too hard. When the cane stalks had the juice squeezed out of them, they were dumped out of the mill onto a wagon. One hired man's responsibility was to level the stalks off so they could get a decent load on the wagon. Then he drove the wagon to the field, unloaded the stalks and came back for more. In drought years they spread the crushed stalks out on the ground until they were dry. Once dried, the stalks were baled and sold for fodder.

Leonard typically asked a lot of his help, and if he asked, he expected to be obeyed. But if the work was dangerous or too hard or if he asked somebody to move something and they thought it was too heavy he simply did it himself. He finally admitted later that his one fault was that he didn't tend to explain everything to someone who was working for him. If he wanted them to do something, he expected obedience without question because sometimes "what he was asking was unexplainable to someone who didn't understand it." He didn't want to waste time. He realized later that he should have been more lenient, but his excuse then was that it was hard for an old man to change his ways!

Marvin continued to complain that the work was too hard. Leonard knew it wasn't, so challenged, "I can unload that whole wagon in fifteen minutes!"

"No you can't!" the 'fella answered.

"Now listen, you just put on a decent load, not so much that it breaks the wagon down and I'll go out and show you." Now usually when they put up a load they just let the stalks pile up and get all tangled. This time the hired man kept the bottom level so he could get more on, and then filled up the wagon normally the rest of the way, so it wouldn't show. But he was doing exactly what Leonard wanted. The stalks were much easier to unload when they weren't all tangled up.

They drove to the field and the 'fella pulled out his watch when Leonard started to work. Leonard worked really hard for a few minutes. He pulled from both sides and managed to get a large portion of the cane stalks unloaded. He was hot and out of breath. No matter what time of year it was, Leonard always wore a full set of long underwear under his overalls and a long-sleeved shirt buttoned all the way to the neck. At that time Leonard was smoking cigarettes so he decided to take a break and roll himself one.

"Hey, that ain't fair, you ain't supposed to stop!" Marvin yelped.

"Just keep your timer going. I'm still working on that fifteen minutes," Leonard replied. He was just getting his breath back, but he was acting like he was loafing. He finished unloading the wagon within the allotted time and had no more trouble with the guy after that.

Even though they hired help every year to make sorghum, the Maasdam mill was essentially a family run business. The family had the most interest in making good sorghum. The trick to good sorghum making was skimming off the impurities—bits of green plant material—at the right time, before the impurities were cooked into the syrup and couldn't be removed. It was easy to make some good sorghum, but it was difficult to get a uniformly good product all season long. There were a thousand different things to watch out for. What you did good one day was wrong the next day. Leonard made his mistakes too, but most of the time he was right, or at least he never admitted that he was wrong!

One season when they were running the mill twenty-four hours a day, Leonard's mother, Henrietta, stayed out in the sorghum house all night to watch the boys cooking—making sure they did not get into any mischief. On this particular night there was a shower in the sky which was affecting the boiling of the sorghum. Henrietta could see the boys weren't getting the skimmings out. The juice kept boiling up green so she finally ran to the house to wake Leonard. "Len! Wake up! We can't get this juice skimmed off! It keeps coming up green and I don't know what to do."

Leonard pulled himself out of bed, struggled into his overalls and walked out to the mill. It sure felt like a thunderstorm was brewing. He wasn't in any hurry and took his time looking the pan over. His mother, her face lined in a permanently worried look, asked over and over again, "What can we do? What can we do?"

Leonard looked some more, checked a few gauges, turned a handle or two and said, "Well..."

"Len, what are we going to do?" She pressed again for an answer, wringing her hands in anxiety.

"Put the fire out."

"Oh my! We can't do that! The juice will spoil and..."

"Okay," he interrupted, ornery as ever, "then go ahead and cook!"

"But it won't work!"

"Then put the fire out!" He didn't want to give her the reason for his solution because he wasn't entirely sure it would work. It was one of those cases that if it didn't work he would have been sitting there "with a mouth full of teeth" and he didn't like that idea at all.

So they put the fire out, took all the juice out of the pan and put it in a barrel. The only way to break the cycle was to take the juice off the heat, let it settle so that the sediment went down and the skimmings could be taken off the top. They put fresh juice in the pan and it cooked up as nicely as could be. The pan had gone out of balance, and the juice was cooking up incorrectly.

The only way to fix it was to empty it and start over.

Arie Lanser was another night time cook down at the sorghum mill. In fact, it was during sorghum making one year that he became acquainted with Johanna Wielard, Gertrude's younger sister. Johanna helped Gertrude prepare the meals for the night time crew and then brought them down to the sorghum house. She brought in Arie's meals and then sat there keeping him company for a few hours.

They eventually got married and Leonard helped them out in various ways. Arie had a small farm and Leonard helped him buy a 640 acre place. He had been hesitant at first because the ground they were looking at was low ground and subject to flooding. Leonard felt good about the whole deal and offered to go in with him fifty-fifty while assuring Arie that, "If there's ever a year when you get such a poor crop so that you can't make it, you can keep the whole crop, make the payment and not pay me back." But Arie never needed it.

When he and Arie first bought the farm east of Lynnville in 1955, it had a lot of timber that Arie wanted to clear. Leonard had been playing with dynamite ever since he was a kid, so he and Arie had a lot of fun packing dynamite into those stumps and blowing them up.

When they were clearing timber, they usually had an axe with them to chop the holes in the stumps for the dynamite. After a while the thrill of the explosion wasn't quite as thrilling any more, so they decided to have some more fun. After digging the hole and packing the dynamite in, the top was nice and smooth. They laid a piece of wood on top so they could watch it fly way up in the air. They were disappointed that it just blew up like the tree stump.

So the next time they decided to use their axe. Sure enough, when she blew, the axe went flying high up into the air, end over end, the axe head glinting in the sunlight as it turned. It was a pretty sight until they realized the axe was flying straight toward their team of horses. Fortunately it missed the animals. They moved the horses a bit farther away and continued their fun with bigger and bigger shots of dynamite. Eventually the axe got such a jolt that the handle broke and they had to buy another one.

Despite the fun he had playing with such dangerous toys, Leonard was always very respectful of the power dynamite had. He had heard of people being killed going to check on dynamite that hadn't gone off. If that happened to him, he waited and went back to it the next day.

Dynamite tended to be pretty expensive. Leonard heard about a ship off the coast of Texas with a load of nitrogen that blew up. So he started experimenting with his nitrogen fertilizer and diesel fuel. He found out that pound for pound his concoction was more powerful than dynamite. He could stuff just two sticks of dynamite in the hole along with nitrogen fertilizer soaked in diesel fuel and get just as big an explosion as he had using much more dynamite. Just one more way to save a few pennies.

∞ ∞ ∞

Although he was a hard boss to work for, Leonard

and the boys with whom he made sorghum also had a lot of fun. While the night shift was at work, the boys who had worked all day fooled around and played all kinds of tricks. And when a new guy started, the boys tried all the jokes out on him.

The boy Leonard hired to replace Jacob was named Joe, and after the first few days of work the boys were ready to try out a few of their favorites on him. "Hey Joe," one of the boys asked while they were sitting around the table after supper, "Can you draw a picture of a bull?"

"Shore," he said, naively drawn into their joke. With the toothpick in his mouth working up and down, he took a piece of cigarette paper and carefully drew a pretty good picture of a bull.

When he had finished, the boy took back his pencil, drew a square around the bull and said, "This is the fence around the pasture. Here, gimme that toothpick in your mouth." He broke it into little pieces and left them in the square next to the bull. "Like I said, this here's the pasture and here's the gate, but the gate is shut. Here's the crick that runs through the pasture, but that's all shut too so he can't get out." Pushing the toothpick pieces around with his grimy pencil stub he continued, "The fence is high enough so he can't jump it, but that bull is gonna get out of that pasture. Now how's he gonna get out of there?"

"Well, he can't. Not unless somebody opens the gate for him. What are those toothpick things in there for?"

With a triumphant grin the boy answered, "That's bull shit!" Everybody laughed. It was always fun to get

Hired Help

Figure 6.1: Leonard (far right) treated the boys to homemade ice cream on the last day of sorghum making, circa 1947.

the new guys!

Now Leonard had been playing tricks on Joe all week too, so the following Monday night Joe thought he'd give Leonard some of his own medicine. "Hey Leonard," he asked him, "Can you draw a bull?"

"Yep," he answered, "You want me to?"

Joe went through the entire joke and Leonard played along the whole way. He kept stalling and asking innocent questions while Joe pushed around the toothpick pieces. Finally Leonard, who had been having a great time, said, "Joe, why are you messing around with that bull shit!" Oh, they had a big laugh.

One year Leonard hired a Dutchman from Holland to work during sorghum making. He couldn't speak English very well but he was one smart guy. He was so smart the other boys didn't know how to handle him whether in tricks or fighting or anything. Pointing to the muscle part of his arm, the Holland boy said to another, "You can hit me on the arm here two or three times and then I can hit you once." The boy hit him on the muscle but since they move around some, it didn't hurt very much. The Hollander hit one glancing blow on another part of their arm and it hurt for two days. They didn't like that very much, so tried all the harder to get him.

But this Holland boy knew all the tricks and he'd get the best of them every time. They put salt in his milk and he would not drink it. The girls served boiled eggs for breakfast, but the Hollander's was raw. He wouldn't touch it. Even Marie tried to fool him. All the jackets hung on nails in the corner so one night she sewed the

Hired Help

sleeves shut on his jacket. He would not touch it. He just went right outside. They never saw him take that jacket out of the house, but eventually he was wearing it and the stitches were taken out. He outsmarted them on everything!

But one time they managed to outsmart him. The haymow in the barn had a chute in it where they threw hay down to the horses. Somehow the boys managed to get just a little hay down in the chute so it looked like it was plugged up. The Dutchman was up there helping them so the boys told him, "The hay chute's plugged up. You're about the only one strong enough to jump on that and loosen it." He bit, and jumped right down as hard as he could. Thunk! He landed on the ground floor of the barn.

∞ ∞ ∞

Leonard's personality was often a study in contrasts. He loved having fun, playing tricks and jokes on people, but if he thought someone was trying to put something over on him, or trying to get by with something, he showed the abrasive side of his personality. Leonard really thought a lot of some of his hired help, and that was one reason why he took five of them to the Chicago World's Fair in 1933. They only had to pay for their food and admission to the fair grounds.

The Maasdams had a 1929 Chevy truck with an enclosed box in which the boys rode, slept, and cooked. As they got closer to Chicago, Leonard stopped once or twice to see if there was any place they could camp. One policeman directed them up one street, then right and then left. Finally Leonard interrupted him and said, "That's Greek to me. What direction is it and how far?"

"About twenty miles south," came the reply.

"Oh, we don't want that far away. We want up close."

The policeman could tell they were greenhorns from the country so he started to emphasize that they were in the heart of Chicago and spaces for campers were costing one thousand dollars a month. He concluded, "It just isn't feasible at all."

"I don't care what it costs," Leonard retorted. "If there's a place, I'd like to know it."

"Well, there is a place near Halsted," the officer finally admitted.

"That's Greek to me. Tell me what direction and how far." It was about a half mile south and east. They zig zagged until they were as far as he said and Leonard stopped again. He asked another officer, "Is there a place for campers anywhere around here?"

"Yeah, just go to the end of the block and turn right a half a block." They drove to the corner and found a vacant lot that charged fifty cents a day to camp. They were only three blocks from the fair grounds!

Leonard and the boys stayed in Chicago from Tuesday until Friday night when they decided to start for home. Admission to the fairgrounds, their eats, streetcar fare and everything else they wanted to buy only came to $3.71 each!

Chapter 7

In the Family Way

After Leonard and Gertrude got married, Gertrude's life on the farm was not an easy one. She had the primary responsibility of caring for the home and the children without the modern conveniences that many farm wives in later years took for granted.

At that time couples didn't talk much about family planning, and Leonard and Gertrude were no exception. Consequently, when Gertrude thought she might be "in the family way" right after their honeymoon, she was unhappy. She was not ready to be a mother yet. When the next month came and she found out she wasn't expecting a baby, she was very relieved.

When two years passed and Gertrude had had three miscarriages, she began to wonder what was going on. She went to the doctor for a checkup and he gave her something that made Leonard comment later, "Boy it sure pepped her up!" Within six months she conceived.

They were still living in Grandpa Mathes' house. Although they had bought the place around the corner, the house there was not fit to live in. Leonard and Gertrude shared his house with their hired man and his wife, Ben and Heretta Verwers, until it could be remodeled. They had two rooms each.

Leonard thought a lot of Ben. He was a good hired man. Since times were tough, Leonard offered to help him get started farming. He and Ben made an agreement that Ben would cash rent Leonard's ground, using Leonard's tractor and implements. For doing all of the work, Ben got to keep half of the profits in addition to earning wages when he was working Leonard's ground.

Leonard also gave Ben one sow and told him he could keep the pigs from it. When the pigs were weaned, Leonard offered to trade sows for any boars he wanted to get rid of. Eventually Ben was able to buy his own equipment and began to farm on his own.

One warm spring evening after dark, before Gertrude was due, she and Leonard decided to go check out how the remodeling was coming along at the other place. Ben's wife overheard some comment that made her think they were going to the hospital. The next morning as usual, Leonard was up first. Heretta came over brimming with curiosity, "Well, where's Gertrude this morning?"

"Well, where do you think?" Leonard answered, knowing full well what she thought, but wanting to have a little fun with her.

"Did you go to the hospital last night?"

At that moment Gertrude walked into the room, her

In the Family Way

still-rounded stomach leading the way. Heretta flushed with embarrassment and didn't know what to say. Leonard and Gertrude just smiled. Leonard was so proud of that baby growing in his wife's womb. He loved to feel it as it moved around.

Finally the time arrived and Gertrude announced that she needed to go to the hospital. They loaded up the car and were on their way to Oskaloosa. As they neared Searsboro, a train was coming down the track so Leonard stopped to let it pass. He thought there was plenty of time. Gertrude gasped nervously, "Leonard, we've got to get there!"

"Now listen," Leonard tried to calm her down. "You just relax and we'll get there in plenty of time."

When they arrived at Abbott hospital in Oskaloosa the attendants were having some kind of a party. The assistant nurse who was attending Gertrude did not have much experience with women in labor. Leonard had been advised to get a little rest so went and slept in the car for a few hours. By the time he got back, things had really moved along. By four in the morning, when the superintendent nurse came by to check Gertrude's progress, it was high time to be calling the doctor. The doctor arrived just in time and before he knew it, Leonard heard his son's cry protesting his entrance into the world. Lawrence Willard Maasdam was born on May 29, 1937.

Being the thrifty Dutchman that he was, Leonard waited until he got home to tell anyone their good news. He didn't want to make a toll call all the way from Oskaloosa!

A few days later, after they had decided to give Lawrence the second name Willard, after Leonard's father's English translation of his middle name, they were eager to share the news. Lane asked Leonard, "Well, what did you name the boy?"

Leonard proudly answered, "Lawrence Willard Maasdam, just like your middle name." Even as he spoke, Leonard watched a cloud go over his father's face, just like somebody had slapped him. He truly hadn't known before that moment how much his father hated his middle name. That was why he always went by L.W. and had legally changed his middle name to the initial "W". Leonard could read his face clearly—*what in the world did you do that for?*

Gertrude tried to nurse Lawrence but didn't have enough milk, so ended up feeding him a bottle. Leonard fed him once in a while and walked the floor with him if he was cranky, but as far as changing diapers, that was women's work! They both learned to recognize the different kinds of cries that Lawrence made by how hard he was crying and in what tone.

Once when Lawrence was less that two years old, he was playing on a scale that had platforms on each side with bee hives sitting on them. Leonard was out in the yard working and suddenly heard Lawrence's terrified screams coming from the scale.

Recognizing the tone of distress and knowing in a moment that Lawrence must have stirred up the bees, Leonard ran to the scene. He saw Lawrence, still holding the stick with which he had been beating the hives, surrounded by a swarm of bees. Thinking, but not caring, that he could get stung too, Leonard did not hesitate. He ran in and rescued his son. Lawrence had gotten stung in several places, but he had learned a lesson in respecting bees!

Nine months after Lawrence was born, Leonard and Gertrude found out they were expecting again. Since they had had such a bad experience with the hospital in Oskaloosa, both Leonard and Gertrude insisted on the doctor coming to their home when the baby was due. So when Darlene Joan was born on November 21, 1938, Gertrude's labor went much more smoothly. The doctor was there for the few hours when he was most needed and then left.

Gertrude was never physically strong. She had always felt somewhat anemic and run down. Before they had children, just caring for her home and garden was more than enough work. Consequently, when Lawrence and Darlene came just eighteen months apart, she was overwhelmed.

She hired a girl to come live with them, sometimes by the week, sometimes by the month. She was usually out of school and wanted to earn some extra money. Gertrude paid her three to four dollars per week.

Gertrude needed her hired girl even more when she became pregnant again nine months after Darlene was born. This time she was not too happy. She had more than she could handle with the two children and now another one was on the way. Marjorie Ellen was born on May 3, 1940. After having three children in such a short time, and because she was in poor health, the doctor advised that she should not have any more children. Gertrude made an appointment with the doctor, and Leonard stood right by her side during the whole operation, even when the doctor's incision laid open her abdomen. He wanted to be there in case anything happened to his wife.

Leonard had faith in the doctors and a stronger faith in God, but he never showed it publicly. Leonard and Gertrude attended various churches in the area, but Gertrude was more of the spiritual leader in the home. She was the one who read Bible stories to the children and prayed out loud before meals. Leonard's faith in God ran a whole lot deeper than most people thought. He knew where the gifts and abilities he had been given came from, but he just couldn't put his feelings into words.

∞ ∞ ∞

One summer when Darlene and Marjorie were four and five, Leonard took his family to the Mathes family reunion in Pella. Unknown to him, their hired girl had been teaching his daughters to sing. Imagine his surprise when his two little girls ran up in front of everyone and sang "Twinkle, Twinkle Little Star." Although he heard them sing many times after that, he was never so proud of them as he was that day.

Lawrence showed character traits of his father even at an early age. They sent him to school when he was five, but he could not take book learning. If Leonard gave him something to work on with his hands he could do it easily. Not getting anywhere in the school system in eight years; Leonard allowed his son to drop out. Education was not important to Leonard. As long as someone was creative with his hands, and willing to work hard, it was enough for him.

Lawrence went to high school for one day. Before the last period of the day, he told his sister Darlene that if he got one more assignment he was never coming back. He got an assignment and never went to school again. He would have considered it if Leonard had been willing to let him play football, but Leonard held firm, "If you want to do that, you can work instead." Lawrence didn't want to go to school if all he had to do was study. Like his father, he was more interested in making money.

Once when Lawrence was still in school, Leonard was going to put on a program at a neighborhood school, showing movies from one of his trips. The show was supposed to start at seven-thirty, but Leonard hadn't gotten home from his business meeting until eight o'clock that night. Lawrence was just a kid, but he got the movie projector set up and showed the pictures all by himself. If he had to use his hands, he could figure things out.

In contrast to their brother, however, both Darlene and Marjorie did well in school. Leonard always thought too much education ruined a person for real work. Hard work and not being lazy were how to succeed. When Darlene announced she wanted to go to high school, he was against it. She spent the summer trying to work very hard so he wouldn't say she couldn't go. Since he never said outright she could or couldn't go, when the fall came, she just went. Because Darlene had gone,

Marjorie went too.

Then, when Darlene graduated from high school, she announced that she wanted to go to college. During her senior year in high school, her boyfriend had been killed in a car accident. When he heard about her plans, Leonard told her, "After what you've been through this year, I'm not going to say you can't go, but I'm not in favor of it." Leonard couldn't see why his daughter needed to go to college, since he had done fine in life with only eight years of schooling.

Darlene attended Central College in Pella and lived at home the second semester after Leonard and Gertrude moved to town. Since Leonard hadn't been in favor of her going, he refused to help very much with tuition. Darlene worked during the summers at various jobs to earn money to pay her college expenses. Leonard went to her graduation, but never gave the impression that he was proud of, or impressed with her educational accomplishments.

After graduating from high school, Marjorie worked at Maytag. She lived in Newton and went home on weekends.

Lawrence farmed with his father for a number of years, but gradually became more and more interested in the construction business, until, eventually, that was his primary vocation.

The level of education of Leonard's three children interestingly showed how he felt about schooling. Lawrence finished the eighth grade; Marjorie, high school; and Darlene, college. In Leonard's mind, the "know-how" each of his children possessed was the same. The amount of education they had made no difference. He felt that education was good for some people, but it wasn't the ultimate. Someone who could not learn, like himself and his son, did not need to feel disadvantaged. To Leonard, the old basic principles were the most important: religion, work, character. He gave God Almighty full credit for any successes he had in life, knowing he never had a good idea in his own strength.

Chapter 8

Moving the Mill

One September Sunday afternoon in 1940, Leonard was in the front room reading the newspaper. The weather had been fair, but was changing rapidly. He noticed heavy wind blowing and heard commotion outdoors so got up to take a look. As he walked toward the kitchen to look out the back door, he noticed their linoleum rug floating fifteen inches in the air! He knew something was going on.

 He ran outside to look for Gertrude and the kids only to find that Gertrude had already rounded them up. They were planning to go to their underground cave, but Leonard didn't think they had enough time so chose the cellar instead. Gertrude had a laundry stove down there and the stove pipe was already smashed absolutely flat! Then Leonard realized the danger they were in—there was a tornado outside that was creating extreme pressures.

After the first wave had quieted down, Leonard cautiously went upstairs to have a look at what had happened. The first wind came from the south and completely removed the hen and brooder houses. All the material from those buildings ended up one quarter of a mile away in the field by the creek.

Then Leonard noticed the wind picking up again, so he went back to the cellar. The second wave, out of the southwest, was the worst of the storm. It tore the roof, the loft, and two sides of the big barn completely down. The loft had been full of hay, and the hay just dropped straight to the ground while most of the building ended up in the ditch by the road.

The third wave tore one of the steel sorghum pans apart and deposited pieces of it over one and a half miles away. Leonard had some hog houses in the field where the center of the storm struck. A number of hogs were killed instantly when boards from their hog houses went straight through them. The strong winds also pulled up one quarter of a mile of web fence, posts and all. The family survived with no injuries, and Leonard even found use for the damaged buildings later.

As Leonard grew older, he began to realize more and more how his whole life had been led by God. He had experienced times of trial and hardship, like his illnesses as a young man and the tornado in 1940. At the time he considered the trials to be a hindrance, but later realized that God worked them out for his own benefit and growth. In other instances he had been led to do the right thing at the right time and realized great success as a result. He couldn't understand why he did

Figure 8.1: The Leonard Maasdam family at ten years, 1944.

the right thing instead of the wrong thing, except that God Almighty was guiding and directing his life.

By the forties Leonard had made sorghum for fifteen years. He was the boss of the whole mill since Fred had said he wasn't interested in making sorghum, and their father wasn't able to any more. When Lane realized that Leonard was the only one of his children interested in making sorghum, he gave the whole business to him and suggested that he move it to his farm a half mile away. Lane gave Leonard three years to move the mill with the condition that everything was to be at his place by the end of 1945.

Leonard spent as much time moving the sorghum mill as his farming responsibilities allowed. In the fall of 1944 he began constructing the actual building of the three story sorghum house. The main area of the mill was called the engine room. It was two stories high and eventually full of machinery, a maze of stairs, catwalks and moving parts. A reporter once described the sorghum mill as a "junkyard come to life."

Showing his Dutch heritage of finding good use for scraps that other people have thrown out, Leonard built most of the mill with used or junk material. His theory was that he could buy heavier duty junk parts, that were much stronger than he needed, for a fraction of the cost of a new part. Because he only used it at, say, one tenth its capacity, it wouldn't wear out. It just ran and ran!

So he salvaged corrugated iron for the walls and roof and he used angle iron from an old wind mill frame to support much of the internal machinery. The tornado

Moving the Mill

that had gone through their farm in 1940 had torn most of the big barn completely off its foundation, but the huge support timbers were still there. Leonard salvaged them and used them to support the second floor of the mill.

Because the timbers were so heavy, they were difficult to put in place and Leonard needed a few men to help him. He had already poured a concrete base on the floor with a huge bolt sticking up. He drilled an equivalent size hole in the bottom of the post so he could set it up and not have the post move around.

The men's muscles strained as they struggled to lift the huge beam in place. They had to get it just right. Finally it seemed good and they let it drop. Leonard let out an excruciating cry, "My finnnngerrr!" Somehow in their struggle he had gotten his right index finger underneath just a little bit. When the post dropped down it took a chunk out of the side of his finger. Now the lump that he had always felt for to tell his right and left hands apart, was gone! The injury took quite a while to heal.

Since the crank shaft on their twenty horse power gasoline engine had broken once too often, the Maasdam's had been using an old Case tractor engine to power the mill. But gasoline was expensive. Leonard began to think about how they had to cut so much wood and buy slack coal (low quality) to heat the furnace to cook the juice. Sometimes the fire burned too hot and the juice scorched and tasted bitter and burned.

Wouldn't it be cheaper, since they already needed the fire, if they would just use it to produce steam in a boiler and use steam to run the mill and cook the sorghum? Because steam can only reach a maximum temperature of 325 degrees at 100 psi, it would be easier to cook the sorghum without burning it. Then, instead of throwing the plummies (sorghum stalks with the juice squeezed out of them) away, they could use them to keep the fire hot. How efficient!

Leonard had heard that the big sugar mills down in the Louisiana sugar cane country were powered by steam engines. He wanted to go down south to take a look. The only problem was that World War II was in full force and gasoline was being strictly rationed. He had tried and tried to get a little extra, but was denied every time, so he finally took a bus trip all the way down south.

Gasoline wasn't the only thing rationed during World War II. White sugar was very much in demand and Leonard and Gertrude could buy only five pounds at a time. When they heard the government was actually going to issue ration coupons for sugar they decided to stock up. Every time they went out selling sorghum to different grocery stores they bought five pounds of sugar. Leonard was installing pipes for running water into the house at that time, and had a trench dug from the barn to the house. He buried jars of sugar in that trench and dug them up when they needed them. Forty-five years later his grandson, John Kramer, found one that had been long forgotten.

Once he got down to Louisiana, renting a car cost far too much money so he went all over on foot, bumming rides when he could. Eventually he found some mills

Moving the Mill

powered with steam. He learned how they used their coils for cooking and how to run the pipes and valves.

He decided that he needed to build a furnace, buy a boiler and a steam engine. But where could he come up with equipment that, as of the 1940's, was outdated? He bought used, of course. At first he bought a steam engine from Grandpa Maasdam's 1850 flour mill for eighteen dollars a ton. He couldn't get the fourteen foot flywheel through the door, however, so dismantled the rest of the machine and waited for them to tear the building down.

In the meantime, he found out about another steam engine that had been used at a saw mill in Red Rock. It had been manufactured by Atlas Engine Works around the turn of the century and only had a five foot flywheel. First used at a factory in Pella and later moved to Red Rock, he bought it for junk price–sixty dollars.

The rim on the fly wheel was eighteen inches wide and over an inch thick. They didn't have any big machinery to hoist it into the building, so the Maasdams carefully loosened the flywheel from the shaft and rolled it from the truck by hand—step by step. They had ropes on each side to keep it from tipping over. They put rollers under the base of the engine, which also weighed a few tons, and gradually got everything moved into place.

Later, a machine shop owner in Pella told Leonard about a one hundred fifty horsepower boiler in an abandoned coal mine. Leonard had the machine shop owner examine the boiler to make sure it was in good condition. Once approved, he bought it for $750.

The boiler was on a brick platform four or five feet from the ground, with brick walls all the way to the ceiling. Leonard tore the brick wall down to the bottom of the boiler, being careful not to damage the bricks. He wanted to use them again to build his own furnace. He had a semi truck back up to the side of the boiler and rolled it right on the truck.

Just getting the thirty-two foot long by eight foot in diameter behemoth iron monster to the farm was difficult enough, but once there, they had to unload it too. They tried to roll it off the truck, but it fell more than rolled and got a dent in it—but not enough to hurt anything.

The boiler hadn't been cared for properly. All of the flues inside were filled with lime. Leonard and his hired man laid it flat on the ground. Leonard was at one end of the tubes and his hired man was at the other. They scraped and scraped to get the lime out; it was awfully hard work.

Once the boiler was cleaned, Leonard knew he had to build his furnace. He had salvaged the fire brick and the grates and everything else from the coal mine, and had looked the whole thing over closely before he tore it down. That was his education in how to build another one. Once again, Leonard didn't want to use book learning. He liked to use his hands and his God-given inventive abilities to figure things out.

He knew he had to build a furnace so big that he could put a firebox in the front, and yet somehow suspend the whole boiler over the furnace so the four inch flues inside could be heated. Once the flues inside the

Moving the Mill

boiler were hot, they in turn heated the water until it began to produce steam.

Leonard needed more bricks for the size furnace he wanted to build. He wasn't about to buy new! A brick kiln had gone out of business in Newton so he bought some fire brick from them. The man selling it was asking ten dollars a load, so Leonard hauled out his biggest trailer, and began loading up bricks!

Leonard laid thousands of fire brick for the furnace, mostly by himself. He figured that if he had hired someone to lay the bricks and install a new boiler it would have cost him ten thousand dollars. Instead he put in a little labor and $820 and the whole thing was ready.

Later that winter Leonard began to build the cookhouse on the top floor of the sorghum mill. In the dead of winter with the temperatures hovering at ten degrees below zero he was putting the roof on.

In the spring of 1945, Leonard began to move the machinery from his father's place to the new building. He knew if he could mechanize the labor part of making sorghum, he could produce a lot more sorghum and make more money, but first he had to survive the first season.

He did manage to make sorghum that fall, but very little. Everything was so new to him and some of his machinery didn't work the way he thought it would. His Dad, his brother Fred, and Uncle Henry all helped him to try to get things running.

Leonard had thought up a method of removing the leaves and other debris from the cane stalks by using parts of several old farm implements. He got a suction

Figure 8.2: Leonard standing next to steaming pans of boiling sorghum juice, circa 1950.

Moving the Mill

fan from a 1913 corn sheller and used it for a blower to push the air upward. Then he used a fan from a 1918 grain separator to blow sideways. He took the shaker from the same machine and remodeled it so it not only shook the cane from side to side, but also up and down. The leaves floated to the top of the traveling mass, got caught in the air channel, and were blown away, while the heavier cane stalks stayed at the bottom. Fred and Leonard built the machine together, but just couldn't get it to work right that first year.

The steam injector from the boiler wasn't working correctly either. Uncle Hen was running the steam engine and firing the furnace, while Leonard tried to cook upstairs. Uncle Hen couldn't keep the steam pressure up high enough and Leonard often drew the steam faster than it could be produced.

One time the steam engine was missing a little push spring. Leonard sent the boys to town to get one, but when they got back, reported that the store didn't have any. Leonard thought for a minute and then pulled the ball point pen out of his pocket. The little spring inside worked perfectly.

By October, things were still not working so finally Fred put in another elevator to bypass the shakers and blowers, and just let the cane go through the mill whole. Lane Maasdam stood on top of the furnace to feed the squeezed cane stalks into the hole on the top, since the full stalk would not go in by itself.

The family didn't have the time to try to make anything else work that first year because they were afraid the cane would freeze in the fields. Even though the seed wasn't quite ripe, they had already chopped it since it was less likely to freeze lying on the ground than standing upright. By the time they got it out of the field there was hardly any juice left in the stalks. All the juice had gone into ripening the seeds. They harvested a little over half a crop the first year, but they were enthused with the new mill and knew it could only get better.

Chapter 9

Mill Improvements

Even in the forties when Leonard moved the mill, the use of sorghum as a sweetener was in decline. If he wanted to purchase machinery to make his mill more efficient and labor-saving, there was none available. Sorghum making was a pioneer industry and sorghum itself was an old-fashioned product, therefore, modern mechanical sorghum manufacturing equipment did not exist. If he wanted mechanization, Leonard had to come up with the ideas himself. Fortunately, he had a lot of ideas for different machinery and was ready to start implementing them.

Leonard had been to Louisiana several more times and was getting to know the sugar cane producers there quite well. One even offered Gertrude and him a place to sleep over night. In fact, driving down there, he stopped at every sugar or sorghum mill along the way to talk and learn. Gertrude went along and waited in the car, usually doing some needlework.

After they started using the corn binder to cut the cane in the field, the hardest job in the mill was unloading the sorghum wagons by hand and throwing the stalks onto the table. On one of his trips to Louisiana, Leonard had seen the huge derricks that the sugar mills used to unload their cane. He had built a wooden derrick at his Dad's place, but was anxious to make a bigger one out of steel. He wanted one to lift an entire three ton load of cane at once and bring it to the starting point in the mill.

He wrote to a derrick company in Minneapolis who sent a salesman out to see Leonard's mill. Since this was during the war years, steel was very expensive and the asking price for the derrick was twelve hundred dollars. That was too much. Leonard accepted the brochures with pictures from the salesman, drove to Des Moines and bought two hundred dollars worth of steel.

If he had had more than an eighth grade education, and was willing to use books, he might have been able to sit down with a pencil and paper and figure out everything he needed to build a derrick. But a formal education he did not have or want. Leonard figured a general plan in his mind, but, because some of the mechanical alignments had to be within a small fraction of an inch to operate reliably, had to keep tinkering with parts until they all worked. God had given him an amazing mechanical talent—something that could never have been obtained solely through education.

Leonard had been learning how to weld as he made the steel cooking pans, but this was a much bigger

Mill Improvements

Figure 9.1: Leonard's "new" sorghum mill with the derrick standing out front, circa 1947. Notice the doors open on the second level to allow steam to escape from the cooking room.

project. He bought an electric welder (they had finally gotten the high voltage lines into their area—before that they had only had thirty-two volts from batteries, with a wind charger and/or gasoline engine to charge them), and began to weld pieces of stock steel and scrap metal together until he had a derrick thirty feet tall. Then he built a boom almost as long to move the sorghum loads and supported it with five cables anchored in a ton of concrete. He knew he needed something strong for the pivot at the top of the derrick so took the secondary drive axle, which was three inches in diameter, from an Avery tractor. Along with it's heavy cast iron bearings, it was placed upright on top of the derrick. That's what the boom swung on.

The Maasdam's had a 1918 Model-T-Ford truck they were no longer using so Leonard salvaged the engine to provide the power for his derrick. He locked the rear end on it, put a shaft on one wheel and attached the tumbling rod to a winch drum which actually wound up the cable that allowed the boom to move up and down. He needed cable strong enough to lift a few tons of cane so he took some from a dragline out of an old coal mine. It took about two weeks to make the derrick and Leonard managed to save enough money by using his own inventive mind to make his time worth five hundred dollars per week.

The corn binder was working acceptably cutting the cane in the field, but it still took the men a long time to strip the leaves and chop the cane into manageable pieces. Leonard started working on the problem and in the early 1950's came up with an idea. If he used a one

Mill Improvements

row chopper like farmers use for corn he could chop the cane down, cut off the heads, cut it into pieces, and load it in a wagon all at the same time.

Leonard used his derrick for about fifteen years, but when they started to use the chopper to cut the cane into small pieces, the sling Leonard used to haul cane from the wagons to the mill wouldn't work. The corn binder left the stalks whole and easy to move. The chopper cut the cane in small pieces that just fell through.

Then he came up with the idea of using the new wagons with hydraulic lifts. When the wagons brought the pieces of cane from the field they simply lifted one end and all the cane spilled out into a neat pile on the ground. One of the hired help pitched it onto the conveyor belt that ran into the plant, leaving as much of the leaves and seeds and other unusable debris on the ground as was possible.

But that was too hard of work, so around 1956 Leonard began implementing another idea. If he could dig a big steel bin almost level with the ground and shape it with sloping sides directed toward a chute at the bottom, with an old corn elevator running underneath it, he could get the sorghum cane all the way from the field into the mill by using one man sitting on a tractor. He picked up some floor plate steel from Vermeer Manufacturing in Pella and began to weld. Like he envisioned, the elevator fed the cane slowly and steadily. The consistent pace greatly reduced the number of times the mill got plugged and needed to be temporarily shut down.

By this time the shaker and blower system of removing dirt, cane leaves and seeds from the chopped cane stalks was working quite well.

These four inventions improved the process of preparing the cane for the mill so much that the work of six or seven men was reduced to one. So in the 60's Leonard thought, *why not make the chopper do two rows and double the amount cut at one time?* His youngest brother, Fred, who also had amazing mechanical abilities, came up with the design for the second chopper that ran on a heavier, lower machine. Fred and his son, Harlan Maasdam, completely redesigned the header on the chopper and kept improving it. The Maasdam family has been working on the choppers ever since so that by the 1990's, one man can cut and load more cane in eight minutes than a crew in the 30's could in a whole day.

Leonard's big steel bin was working well too, but with a two row chopper, it wasn't as big as he wanted, and his original idea of a bin with sloping sides sometimes caused the cane to feed too quickly and plug up. So he and his son-in-law, Charles Kramer, made an even bigger one, this time with square sides—eight feet wide, six feet deep and thirty feet long—that held three wagon loads full of cane. He installed a conveyor belt at the bottom that, like a large forage wagon, carried the cane pieces into the plant at a rate of one and a half inches per minute.

Leonard's youngest daughter, Marjorie, had married Charles Kramer in 1960. Charles worked in a factory the first few years of their marriage, until one day, when they were at Leonard's house in Pella, Leonard offered to help Charles get started farming. Charles was very interested, but didn't have the money. Leonard went to the bank, set up an account where Charles could borrow what he needed, and made the arrangements that Charles would pay him back when he started making a profit.

Charles began learning to make sorghum the first year he moved to the farm. By the second year, Leonard saw that his son-in-law was a good worker and wanted him as a partner in the sorghum mill. As he told other partners in later years, Leonard made it clear to Charles, "You go in with nothin', you go out with nothin'." Leonard didn't want any money from Charles for his partnership, and as long as Charles stayed in the business, he earned a percentage of the profits. But if Charles decided he wanted out, or was booted out, he couldn't take anything with him. As Leonard grew older, Charles ran the entire sorghum operation.

With ten to twelve tons of cane in the bin, Leonard and Charles did not want any problems with the chain breaking on the conveyor when the bin was full. Neither relished the idea of needing to take all the cane out by hand. Leonard called on Vermeer's once more. They had heavy duty digger chains that they simply replaced when the rollers wore too much. Vermeer's gave him the chains for junk. They would have cost twenty to twenty-five dollars a foot if he had purchased them new. He bought new pins and bushings for the chain for eighty dollars and spent a week repairing the old chain. When he was finished it was as good as new and provided years of trouble free use.

He knew he needed a heavy gear box to run that

heavy duty chain—one that would be able to handle that much weight. J.I. Case Company had introduced a slice baler in the 1930's that had just the gearbox he was looking for. He used it for his final reducing gear and it's been operating for over twenty-five years. Later, Charles put an auger in the front of the bin instead of a conveyor to move the cane pieces more easily without getting plugged up.

Once the cane stalks came through the blowers, they were ready for the machine that gave the sorghum mill it's name—the mills. As the stalks moved along the conveyor toward the first mill, long flailing metal teeth helped distribute and control the flow of cane. Just before they entered the first press, the pieces were crushed by a large metal roller. From there, they were sent through a series of three mill presses, which were pushed by thirty tons of weight each, totaling sixty thousand pounds of pressure. The mills pulverized the stalks and squeezed out all of the liquid so that what was left was dry enough to burn in the furnace.

Next, the sticky green juice was collected in six hundred gallon holding tanks before going to the top floor for the evaporation and cooking process. The raw juice flowed through a series of three settling and evaporating pans, each twenty feet long by five feet wide. Leonard built these huge tanks and pans from new sheets of steel that he welded together.

To begin the purification process, the juice was heated to 180 degrees in the first pan, and filtered between pans to remove impurities. The juice was allowed to stand in each pan for about an hour. Impurities were skimmed

Mill Improvements

from the top of each pan during this time, while the heavier sediment found in the juice was allowed to settle on the bottom. Only the clean juice was pumped from one tank to the next. The sediment at the bottom of each tank was pumped into yet another tank where they were still able to salvage a bit more juice.

Finally the juice was pumped through a fine copper mesh filter and into the finishing pan where it was cooked at 225 degrees for two to three hours until it reached proper viscosity and the sugar content was increased from the initial 11–15 percent to 80 percent. It takes seven to nine gallons of juice, depending on its sugar content, to make one gallon of sorghum syrup.

From the final cooking pan, the sorghum was moved to a cooling device, a series of rotating cups that lifted the warm syrup from the pan, pouring it through the air to accelerate it's cooling. Leonard knew he needed a very low gear to drive the paddle that lifted the sorghum so he looked into using a cream separator. The gear between the handle and the spindle of the cream separator was too high of a speed so he put a V-pulley on the spindle and used it in reverse. Now he had a low reducing gear to help cool his sorghum.

Once the sorghum was cooled, it was sent through a network of pipes into the bottling and labeling room. Leonard actually spent two hundred dollars on a new automatic bottling device that filled each jar or plastic container to the correct weight. This unit was a great improvement over the hand spigot, for the spigot had to be turned on and off manually with every jar. And sometimes it didn't get turned off soon enough! Each jar was finished with a bright red "Maasdam Sorghum" label glued on by hand with cornstarch glue. Once the jar was packed in a shipping box, it was ready for the customer. The bottling and labeling operates today pretty much unchanged from thirty years ago.

Chapter 10

Double or Nothing

Leonard had the time to design and implement these mechanical improvements to the sorghum mill because he had retired from active farming in 1949 at forty-six years of age. By that time he had acquired four hundred acres of ground and was working long hours to farm it. More and more, he had been coming to the realization that farming wasn't very interesting to him any more. In fact, it was the least interesting thing in which he was involved.

He did some checking around and found that he could cash rent the ground to tenants and receive almost the same amount of income from it without doing any work himself. He saw no reason to work so hard, because financially he already had everything he needed. When he was younger, Leonard had set out to earn as much money as he could, but that was changing.

Being a Dutchman, it was difficult for Leonard to

part with his hard-earned pennies. As he grew older, however, he often loaned money to people who asked him for help, or gave money outright when someone was in real need. His ability to "read" people helped him make these decisions. When Gertrude heard about a woman whose husband had left her with three small children at home, she told Leonard about the situation and they decided to help her. They put her through college and were such a support to her that eventually her children started calling Leonard "Pappy." They remained life-long friends.

By retiring from full-time farming, Leonard could take Gertrude and the kids on trips to Texas in the winter if he wanted to. They ended up traveling quite a bit, both with the children and without, making trips to many states, Japan, Israel and Europe.

Leonard and Gertrude made a special trip to California in the mid-sixties after the three children had married and moved away. Prior to 1964 all paper money was backed by silver, and silver certificate dollar bills were the government's guarantee. Now the government was going off the silver standard, and was calling in all their silver certificate dollar bills. Leonard had acquired a lot of these bills over the years and planned to convert them to silver bars for $1.29 an ounce. He went to the local bank and they said they couldn't handle them. They would have to be sent to San Francisco or Philadelphia. So Leonard decided to handle it himself.

When the Maasdam's got to the San Francisco mint, there was a long line of people waiting to turn in their bills. The individuals turned in their money, received a receipt, handed it to a guard, and waited for him to return with their silver. One man ahead of Leonard received a large number of bars and was carrying them in his hands like cord wood. As he was walking across the street to his car, they started slipping and fell everywhere. Leonard had filled a few heavy duty satchels when he left the mint and it was all he could do to carry them the three or four blocks to the car. He gave the kids silver chips for Christmas and hid the rest.

∞   ∞   ∞

A few years before retiring, Leonard built a modern seven room house just down the road from the sorghum mill so his tenant could live on the home place. The project took about one year. He started by digging the basement with the horses and a scraper. He could have hired the work done with machinery, but that would have cost money and he was too stingy for that.

When it came to actually constructing the house Leonard thought new lumber was too expensive. He had just bought another farm across the river, and in the winter hired a few boys to tear the house down. They left the room with the wood stove in it intact, and sat there for days taking nails out of boards and stacking them up. He paid the boys fifty cents a day. That was a lot cheaper than new lumber.

He did most of the work himself except for the framing, plastering, and furnace installation. He dug the basement, laid the brick, poured the cement floors, did all the building, plumbing, finishing and painting. They moved in during the summer of 1948.

In fact, Leonard did have extra time and in February 1951, he took Gertrude on a little trip to California. He had heard Walter O'Keef's "Double or Nothing" radio program and really wanted to get on it. They had three shows and people had to stand in line at the door to get in. He and Gertrude were near the end of the line and a man from the show said they probably wouldn't get in because so many people were ahead of them. The Maasdam's stubbornly waited in line and sure enough, they were the last ones in the building.

Before the show started Walter O'Keef walked down the aisles and asked what people's occupations were. Leonard was determined to get on that show, and so, even though he was way off to the side, when Walter asked who he had in his audience, Leonard stood up and spoke in a loud clear voice, "a farmer from Ioway." He had dressed up for the occasion, putting on a clean pair of overalls.

Walter looked right up at him and said in his nasal announcer's voice, "Oh, a farmer from Iowa! Go on up." Before the actual game started, the announcer interviewed the players. Each time he asked Leonard a question, he didn't get a straight answer. Leonard always answered in a funny way, partly on purpose, but partly because he couldn't hear very well.

Walter didn't know what to think. "This is the most unusual contestant I've faced in many a year, in the person of Leonard John Maasdam. Leonard, welcome to the program."

"Thank-you."

"You know hereafter, whenever I think of a farmer,

I'll think of you. You're a moose of a man. How tall are you anyway?"

"About six foot three and a half."

"And you've been tilling the soil all of your life?"

"Yes, I have, outside of when I was a baby and then I don't know."

"How many teeth did you have when you were a baby?"

"I wasn't able to count."

"You couldn't count then. How many Cadillacs do you have, Leonard?"

"I don't know."

"You mean it's that good in Iowa that you don't know how many Cadillacs you have?"

"Oh... I thought you said cavities." The audience roared with laughter.

"Oh no, no. Well what kind of stuff do you farm? What do you specialize in?"

"Well I specialize right now, particular, in making homemade sorghum."

"Homemade sorghum? Well now, I'm a city fellow, Leonard, how do you make homemade sorghum?"

"Well, you raise lots of cane to start with!"

"You've got to be pulling my leg! I think somebody must have written some material for you Leonard! What do you do with your sorghum once you've raised a lot of cane?"

"Well, I manufacture it into a syrup so the public will buy it. And then I go and peddle it out to the grocery stores."

"I see. How many children do you have, Leonard?"

"Three."

"Are they farmers?"

"They're hardly old enough, but they're helping me as best they can." More laughter.

"Leonard, I was just wondering, when you were standing in some misty dawn in a far pasture, did you ever think that you were going to stand up in Hollywood and make millions of people laugh over the radio?"

"No, not at all, but as far as misty, we don't have the fog that you folks have."

Walter commented to the delighted audience, "You know this is a very dangerous 'fella for me to have up here! Let me ask you this, how did you meet Mrs. Maasdam, your wife?"

"Well, sir, I was in town and seen a nice looking girl with some of her friends. I didn't know who they was and so started talking to her. Well one thing led to another and she was ready to go home and so I took her home. She was agreeable to that and there we was. I'll tell you another thing..."

"You'll tell me another thing, I bet you will!"

"After I got her home I asked her for another date and just went on from there. Yeah...no"

Leonard had been planning to tell a story, but remembered just in time that all the folks at home were listening, and he didn't want to say that. Instead he said, "You know, it's just like olives in a bottle."

Walter doubtfully repeated, "Like...olives in a bottle?" He had no idea what was coming, and didn't know if he wanted to!

"Yeah, you know the first one is hard to get and the

rest come easy." The crowd howled with laughter!

"Leonard, let me tell you one thing, in almost four years of doing this, I've never had a more enjoyable contestant than you." The audience's applause echoed his statement. Campbell's soup was the sponsor of the "Double or Nothing" program so Walter asked, "Leonard what is your favorite kind of Campbell's soup?"

"Pork and Beans in tomato sauce."

"In that case, Mr Maasdam, we'll send you a case of jellied sorghum."

"That's good to put in with it! That's why I like it!"

"You're the most natural talent on the microphone since Marconi, believe me."

"I don't know, it's my first time here."

"Well all right, now listen to this. Let's get started with the show. Here's the grand prize question, Leonard. The Chinese show respect by how many courses they serve at a meal. In order to show the highest respect, how many courses would the Chinese serve at a dinner?"

"Well I guess I'm not a big shot, because they only served two courses to me over in China Town!"

"This is the first time I ever wished this program ran for a full hour! Well, what would you guess, Leonard?"

"Two!"

"All right, what category do you want? Shopkeepers? About running a store?"

"Well that depends what kind of a shop you have. If it's a farm shop, okay."

"Let me ask you the first question for two dollars. If

you sell direct to the consumer, you're a what, beginning with the letter 'R'?"

"Well, you're a retailer."

"That's it. Now, what is the opposite of a retailer?"

"A consumer."

"I was gonna say wholesaler, but you're better. The six dollar question for Campbell's soup, what does FOB mean?"

"Cash on Delivery!"

"FOB means Freight on Board, so you have won twenty bucks. Do you want to go double or nothing?"

"I'll try."

"Let me ask you this, somebody in the men's clothing business is a what, starting with 'H'? They get to the White House and they play the piano and what do they do? You buy your clothes and shirts from them?"

To make the best show possible, an employee from the "Double or Nothing" program was standing behind Leonard whispering the answers for him on any questions he hesitated on. But Leonard, being hard of hearing, couldn't understand what he was saying!

"It's something like husherberries, but I don't know," Leonard answered.

"That's it, haberdasher! You've won thirty dollars!" The band struck up the "Double or Nothing" theme song and the show was over. It didn't seem to matter whether or not Leonard answered the questions correctly, just as long as the show was entertaining.

Later that year, in October, Leonard received an invitation to appear on the "Double or Nothing" radio program again, all expenses paid.

"I'm very happy to have our next contestant up here. And those of you who are faithful listeners will remember a gentleman we had here last February, a farmer from Lynnville, Iowa, Leonard Maasdam. Leonard, when you were here before, you were one of the most interesting contestants we have ever had, talking about your sorghum business back in Iowa. How's it going, Leonard?"

"It's going pretty good, Walter." By his second time on the show Leonard was feeling pretty comfortable and called the announcer by his first name.

"Leonard, if I were ever going to make a movie and needed to cast the part of a farmer, you'd be the 'fella. Did you ever consider going to the movies, Leonard?"

"Well, last time after I got off this program, people on the street were asking, 'What happened? It sounded like there was a riot in there.' Well, I didn't know them from Adam. It made me feel so foolish."

"You shouldn't feel foolish. You made the people laugh. You said some funny things. We're very happy to have you here. What kind of a farming season have you had, Leonard?"

"Well, back in Ioway we've had a cold, wet season for growing crops."

"In other words, your dollar bills aren't green this year, they're a pallid brown?"

"Well, dollar bills we don't grow, we have to grow something else to start with."

"My information says that you came out on the airplane. Did you talk to the hostess on the airplane?"

"You bet..."

"I'll bet you did, you rascal," Walter interrupted. "What did you talk to her about, did you tell her any jokes?"

"Well, I didn't tell her any jokes, I simply asked her a question."

"Is it the sort of question I might ask somebody here?"

"I think so."

"Well then," he drawled, "go right ahead!"

"My wife and I had an argument before we left home and she had to have it settled before I got home. She said coconuts grew on vines and I said they growed on bushes. We couldn't get it settled. Well, the hostess didn't even have time to answer before one of the passengers said they grow on trees."

"Why, certainly they grow on trees!"

"Well, any monkey knows that, Walter!" The audience erupted into laughter again.

"I certainly walked right into that one, didn't I? That's all right. Now I'd like to know what happened. I understand the last time you were on 'Double or Nothing' you had a record made, did you play that record back home?"

"Well, I played it at the Fourth of July celebration in Pella, Ioway. That's where they make the Pella cookies and Pella bologna."

"I didn't know that! As I recall you're an active sorghum farmer. Now I didn't know what sorghum was, but it's a wonderful syrup on pancakes, isn't it? Now why don't you explain to some of these hillbillies out here what sorghum is and how you make it."

"Now you take the hillbillies in Missouri, they know what sorghum is! Well, you have to raise lots of cane to start with."

"Well, Leonard, we'd like to see if you can win some money, what's your favorite kind of Campbell's soup?"

"Oh, chicken noodle."

"We'll send you a free case. Now what category?"

"Milk."

"A farmer, shall we bring a cow in to make you feel at home, Leonard? All right, a two dollar question for Campbell's, taking the cream off milk leaves the milk called what?"

"Skim milk."

"A four dollar question for Campbell's Soup, the milk in an infant's bottle is made so that it is proportioned correctly for it's stomach. This is called what, starting with 'F'? Do they have that back in Iowa?"

"Well I imagine you mean formula."

"Yeah, that's what I meant. A six dollar question for Campbell's Soup, what's the difference between condensed and evaporated milk?"

"Condensed milk has the water taken out and evaporated milk has sugar added to it."

"Now a ten dollar question for Campbell's Soup, the quality of milk is judged by it's quantity of what?"

"Butterfat."

"Do you have cows, Leonard?"

"We have seven or eight."

"Don't you know how many you have?"

"Well, my boy does most of the milking. We only milk about five. I have seven now, but I might have eight when I get back home!"

"I can't argue with you there, do you want to go double or nothing for twenty bucks?"

"I'll try."

"Okay, for Campbell's Soup, after cleaning the churn thoroughly, the liquid that remains is called what?"

"Buttermilk!"

"Right, and now for forty dollars, here's your opening joke coming back to roost. What kind of tropical fruit is filled with milk?"

Leonard laughed, "A coconut!"

"You've won forty dollars! Congratulations!"

The theme music played again to close out the program. Leonard went back to the farm, although he was no longer a full-time farmer.

Chapter 11

The Digging Machine

After they moved into the new house in the winter of 1951, Leonard started tinkering with machinery again—but not for the sorghum mill this time. He got to thinking about how much work it was to dig trenches for tile to drain the wet places in his fields. He'd been doing it ever since he was a kid, digging the trenches for his Dad by hand. He had seen the great big digging machines that were ten to twelve feet high and self-propelled, but knew they weren't practical for his needs. To keep himself out of mischief, he decided to try to make one that was small enough so he could pull it behind his own tractor.

He started tinkering with old farm machinery, combining parts from a manure spreader, a grain threshing machine, a corn elevator, hay hoist and a Model-T-Ford. He had the idea that he wanted to be able to hitch it to the back of a tractor and use the power take-off in the

Figure 11.1: Leonard's POW-R-DITCHER, circa 1952.

tractor to make it run. He arranged gears and sprockets on a shaft and welded cutter teeth to it. It had a chain that cut into the ground, pulling the rounded teeth up with a cup or two of dirt on each one. As the chain reached the top, the load of dirt emptied onto an elevator that threw the dirt off to the side.

He built the teeth out of a Model-T-Ford truck rear-end spring that was about four inches wide. It was a hard steel and held a good edge, he thought. He tore the springs out of the Ford, pounded them into shape, put them on and they looked great. Eventually he took the machine out in the field and the teeth worked well there too. They never wore out. Except when he hit a rock, they broke like glass! Leonard was not concerned. He just saved the pieces and in the evening he drove home and welded them together again.

Leonard put a winch drum in the front of the tractor, the kind used when winding up a cable, along with a ratchet from a manure spreader. This is how he could make the tractor move at a slow enough pace while still being able to convert the total power available in the engine into the digging process. At full speed the tractor could power the ditcher to dig four to five feet per minute. The three lower notches were proportionally slower.

Leonard also had one more gear up by the crank, where he could raise and lower the boom to get the right depth for the ditch, depending on the grade of the land. After spending about two hundred dollars on new parts and about two weeks of time, Leonard had something that actually dug a ditch.

Soon after Leonard began tinkering with the machine, he began to realize that it had distinct commercial possibilities. He approached a local blacksmith shop in Sully with part of his idea to see if the owner was interested. Leonard walked into his shop and casually mentioned, "What would you think about making me some cutter teeth?" He wanted to feel out what kind of interest the guy might have in a project.

Wiping his grimy hand on his overalls, the blacksmith peered up at Leonard, "What you want me to make one for? You can buy 'em much cheaper. It's pretty stupid to pay somebody to make something when you can buy it yourself."

Leonard didn't bother one minute more with the man. He didn't need to be made fun of. He had heard of another guy by the name of Gary Vermeer in Pella whose company, Vermeer Manufacturing, was making a few gadgets to make farming a little easier. He went to him next.

He knew one thing. He did not want to go to any of the big factories. He had heard enough stories about inventors who essentially had their inventions stolen away from them without earning any royalties. A little guy would show his idea to a big farm implement manufacturing outfit and they just laughed at him. But the next year they were selling a product just like he had showed them. Leonard was determined that that wasn't going to happen to him, so he went and talked to Gary Vermeer.

At first, Gary was skeptical. "Leonard," he said, "I had a guy come to me with an idea for a digging machine like you're describing and it wouldn't even dig. You're saying you've only worked on this thing for two weeks and it works?"

"Yeah, and I'd love to show it to you!"

"Could it be trailer mounted? I'm not interested in it if we have to have different attachments for all the different tractors."

"No... I don't think so... wait a minute. I could easily put a couple of wheels on her!" Leonard was getting excited.

"Well, when can I see it?"

"Just come over tomorrow."

"We just bought an airplane. Is there any place we

The Digging Machine

could land over there?"

"We got lots of stubble fields!"

Gary and his cousin, Ralph, came out and looked the thing over. They took it out in the field and dug a trench with it, and it treated them just fine. Then they got busy. Leonard had used mostly junk and used parts, so, using his original, they came up with a few prototypes using regular parts. They let farmers around Pella use the prototypes for a year to work out any problems before they actually started selling them through their dealerships.

Vermeer Manufacturing sold implements through dealerships across the country. Gary decided the best way to introduce a new machine that no one had ever seen before, was by demonstration. He needed someone that was willing to travel, was thoroughly familiar with the machine, could put on a good show, and knew how to handle people. Leonard was the obvious and perfect choice. So in the spring of 1952, Leonard started demonstrating his invention.

Leonard's first trip lasted about a month and covered many small towns in Iowa and Minnesota. On one of his first demonstrations, Leonard was running the ditching machine from the seat of the tractor. Someone else was taking the crumbs of dirt out of the trench and laying the tile behind him.

"Say, Leonard," he suggested, "why don't you fix it so I don't have to take the crumbs out all the time?"

Leonard had been thinking how well everything was going, but when he heard that he thought, *Whoop, maybe I'd better try laying the tile myself.* He got back there and realized his assistant was right. The tiling wasn't so much fun from that end of the tractor.

That was in the morning. After their dinner at noon, Leonard attached a piece of scrap iron to the back of the machine. It was the width of the ditch and curled up a little on the edges. The chain pulled the iron along behind the little buckets and made a cleaner ditch. They laid tile right up to the end of the ditch, and when the last bucket was pulled out, the dirt behind the crumber fell on top of the last tile.

For the next two springs Leonard went on additional month-long demonstrating trips. He traveled all the way from New Orleans to North Dakota and down to the Carolinas. He even did a short spurt in Canada. As he showed the machine to both dealers and farmers, he developed a "program" where he gradually showed all the different things the machine could do. To keep audience attention for the full demonstration, he would not show all of the capabilities of the machine right away.

Since it was spring, the conditions for digging trenches were not ideal. In some spots, the ground was soggy with mud, other places the soil was so sandy it caved in, and farther north frost was still in the ground. But Leonard knew how to operate the machine in all these conditions.

∞   ∞   ∞

Early one spring in Iowa, Leonard was performing a ditch digging demonstration in muddy ground. His

The Digging Machine

machine did not work very well in muddy ground and he knew it. That was one of its weak points. He would be digging along and the dirt would get so sticky it balled up and clung to the buckets, making progress impossible.

Within the first five minutes of running the machine, Leonard noticed that the dirt was getting very sticky. He knew it would bind soon if he didn't do something, so he stopped the machine, just like it was part of the program, and innocently asked, "Any questions?" He answered the questions all the while keeping an eye on his ditch. Since the purpose of laying tile is to drain water off soggy ground, the soil was saturated and his ditch had filled with water. That was just what he had been waiting for. As the water came in and filled up the ditch it cleaned off the buckets until everything was ready to go again. When Leonard saw the water he asked, "Well, do you want to see her run some more?"

That trick never failed to impress the farmers. "Boy," they said, "if that machine will dig through that mess, it will dig through anything." But they had no idea how close Leonard was to getting stuck. Most of the time, the conditions were not that extreme, as the farmers well knew.

Early in the spring, Leonard only put on demonstrations on the grounds of the implement dealer's showroom. But when the conditions were actually fit to lay tile, he went to a farm. It was his policy to avoid surprises, so whenever they were scheduled to dig at a farm he looked it over ahead of time so he knew what to expect.

The soil conservation agents usually attended the demonstrations since they helped pay for laying farm tile. Consequently, they were very interested in seeing if this machine would work.

One young farmer in Illinois volunteered his field for a tiling demonstration hoping to get fifteen hundred tile, over a quarter mile, laid for free. Leonard drove over in the morning to check out the place, and noticed right away he was an overbearing fellow. As soon as he met him, the guy was pushing him. "You ready to start tiling now?"

"Well," Leonard replied, "the soil conservation 'fellas have to approve the tiling and we're here so they can see what the machine can do, and they ain't coming 'til after dinner." The conservation agents were responsible for staking out and approving where all tile was laid.

"Just go ahead and get started anyway."

"No sir," Leonard replied firmly, "I'm here for the soil conservationists and I know what happens when you cross them the wrong way. The tiles ain't staked out and we're not doing nothin' 'til they come."

"Well, be sure you're here early then."

Leonard went back at noon. The soil conservation agents were supposed to be there at one o'clock, but were a little late. As soon as they arrived the young farmer was trying to hurry them up. When you try to hurry people up, they tend to go that much slower. Finally the field was staked out and Leonard started his digging machine.

As was his custom, he began slowly. He didn't want to show everything he had in the first five minutes.

The Digging Machine 113

His pace wasn't fast enough for this obnoxious young farmer. He kept motioning Leonard to go faster, go faster. Leonard shook his head and kept the ditcher in the lowest speed. After a while Leonard observed that the crowd of neighboring farmers and soil conservationists had noticed the friction between them. Never one to miss an opportunity for a show, he decided to have some fun.

After he had dug one to two hundred feet he cranked up the power one notch. The 'fella was still motioning him to go faster, faster. Leonard shook his head and kept the machine moving about half speed. They were laying the tile and everything was going smoothly on the nice level ground.

When the ground is level, running a ditching machine is a fairly simple task. The stakes mark where the trench is to be dug and a string stretched between them at a certain height shows the depth of the trench. A rod attached to the back of the crumber with a cross-bar on top follows the string so the driver can adjust the depth of the digger. When the ground is uneven, however, the depth of the digger needs to be adjusted constantly.

Leonard was moving his digging machine along at half speed when the impatient young farmer walked up to him and motioned for him to stop. "If we're going to buy this here machine I'd sure like to try out a little farmin' with it," he said, with a facade of politeness.

Since it was the farmer's tractor, Leonard pleasantly replied, "With all pleasure, you may have it."

It just so happened that just ahead of the tractor the ground had a distinct dip in it. The first thing the young farmer did was to throttle the tractor wide open so it was going five feet a minute. Within ten seconds the front wheels of the tractor hit a depression in the ground. The draw bar went up and that pushed the ditcher higher than the string guide. Because he had never run the machine before and he was going so fast, the young farmer had no idea what to do to correct himself. He rammed the controls one way and realized that was wrong; then rammed them the other way. Just as he got the crossbar aligned with the string the back wheels of the tractor went into the depression and the whole process was reversed.

When Leonard motioned him to stop the tractor, the crossbar was a foot below the string, and the ditch was terribly uneven. They had to even out the bottom of the ditch by hand. Leonard was laughing hard on the inside, but straight-faced on the outside. Once he had helped the young farmer get everything straightened out, the guy rammed the tractor into high gear once again.

The 'fella laying the tile straddled the ditch just after it had been dug. He carried a long stick with a hook on the end that allowed him to move the tile around once it was dropped in the hole until it fit into the previous one.

This farmer had the ditcher digging at five feet a minute again, and the man laying the tile couldn't keep up. The tractor was more than forty feet in front of him and Leonard knew exactly what was going to happen. The ditch started caving in and the tile wasn't in yet. The 'fella yelled back at Leonard, "Help me back it up so we can do it over!"

The Digging Machine

Leonard seriously answered, "We can't back up. The ditch is there and the front tires will go right in the ditch." So they ended up digging that whole section by hand in order to lay the tiles.

∞ ∞ ∞

Another time, Leonard was working with the territory salesman in Illinois for a few days. The first day Leonard was running the demonstration and going through his program telling about the machine. He had gone through most of his selling points and could see the crowd was losing interest. So he said, "Say, do you want to see the weak points of this machine?" The crowd perked up right away as he began to explain how the power take-off on the machine wasn't exactly centered on the tractor and if you turned one way it got too tight, but if you turned the other way it might slip apart. There were a couple other little things that an operator needed to know if he was going to run the machine.

That night in the motel, the territory salesman said to Leonard, "I don't like you talking about the weak points of this machine. Don't say that anymore."

"But, them are things they should know!"

"Don't mention it anymore."

Leonard continued to argue, but the salesman was adamant so Leonard finally agreed, "Okay, tomorrow we'll do it your way."

The next day's demonstration was supposed to start in the afternoon, but by nine o'clock in the morning a crowd of people had already gathered. They were experiencing poor conditions for tiling that spring with sandy soil and trenches caving in. The farmers had a lot of questions and that's why they were there early, looking for answers.

Leonard did just exactly as he had been instructed. When they asked a hard question, he didn't answer it directly and started talking about something else as soon as he could. After a while the farmers actually got hostile. They wanted answers! Leonard took it as far as he could and then said smoothly, "Well, it just so happens that the salesman for the territory is here and I'll turn it over to him."

The farmers swarmed all over the poor salesman and within five minutes he was completely stumped. He said, "Leonard, you take over." And within another five minutes Leonard had them completely calmed down.

This demonstration was in eastern Illinois right near a big race track across the state line in Indiana. Leonard started talking calmly to the irate farmers, "Now listen, you take that race track for example. If you get a car that's A-1 for racing and the fastest on the tracks, where will you try that machine out? Will you try it out by racing? You're a darn fool if you do. You'll take it in the back pasture where no one can see you, so you can figure out how to handle it. That's the same way with this machine. Don't try it first at maximum depth and full speed. Go where you have good digging so you can get used to the machine and learn which way is up and which way is down and how to handle it if the conditions are muddy or sandy or whatever. And if it's sandy make sure you get the tile in there right fast behind the tractor before the trench caves in."

That afternoon the men were in a field digging a trench. The 'fella laying the tile was having trouble keeping up with Leonard, so Leonard suggested they trade jobs for a while. With the ease of an expert, he laid the tile in, hooked them around and banged them together. Before long he was caught up. It was getting late in the day and the territory salesman was getting ready to leave. When he was about twenty feet away Leonard called him back. "Now, did I do good today, or didn't I?" he asked.

The salesman nodded and said, "It's all yours, Leonard."

No matter where he was demonstrating, there was one question that Leonard was always asked. And he loved to answer it. After he had gone through his whole sales program, some young smart aleck would ask, "But does this machine do everything a Buckeye machine can do?"

Leonard had originally gotten the idea for the ditching machine from the big Buckeye digger that construction companies used. It was ten to twelve feet high and cost thousands of dollars; it was impractical for an individual farmer to buy.

Leonard immediately responded, "No sir, it will not!" and then stopped. He could feel the whole audience wondering what he was going to say next. He continued, "Well, the difference between thirteen hundred dollars and thirteen thousand dollars, that's your answer." There wasn't one time that the answer didn't stop them.

As the dealers became more familiar with the machines, they began to demonstrate the machines themselves. Leonard continued to demonstrate his machine around Pella every year and for other special occasions. His manager at Vermeer's was a "town guy" as Leonard called him. He was a good salesman but didn't know how to actually operate the machine. So every time they sold a machine locally or one needed repair, they called Leonard.

One man who lived in What Cheer had bought one of their machines and Leonard's manager hated to work with him. He was an argumentative know-it-all. It had to be his way or no way. So when he called Vermeer's asking for help with his ditcher, Leonard was sent out on the job. He was pretty ornery himself and knew how to handle guys like that. As soon as Leonard got out of the truck the guy was on to him. "I had this thing in the shed all winter and when I took it out this spring it made such a rough ditch I couldn't do nothing with it. The ground isn't too wet, or too sandy or nothin'. Why won't it work?"

Leonard began to look the whole machine over starting at the front end. He was immediately interrupted, "What you looking here for? It's at the back end. This ain't got nothing to do with it!"

The more he argued the more Leonard loved to argue! Finally Leonard told him, "Sometimes the most insignificant little thing can cause the trouble." He continued to do a thorough job of looking over the whole machine, much to the farmer's frustration. Finally Leonard had stalled as long as he could and said, "Well,

The Digging Machine

start it up." Before the machine had dug five feet he knew he had to adjust the crumber. "Stop the machine!" he yelled over the noise of the tractor. He started adjusting the crumber when he was interrupted.

"Don't adjust that! That's got to stay!"

"Well, okay," Leonard responded. "Go ahead and run it then."

"Well, it won't work. It's making a rough ditch."

"Okay, then let me adjust this thing!"

Leonard couldn't believe the guy still wanted to stop him! Finally he adjusted the crumber just a little bit and ordered the farmer to start the machine again. He noticed right away the ditch was improving so ordered him to stop once more. He adjusted the crumber again and the ditch was just as smooth as it could be. The know-it-all didn't know what to say and that's just what Leonard wanted.

∞   ∞   ∞

Another time Leonard was given the job of setting up and demonstrating a machine in Fairfield. Leonard knew that he was not always very well liked by people because when he wanted something done a certain way, he insisted on it. His ditching machine was designed to use the power take-off on the tractor. The power take-off was constructed with a shield over top of it, and a telescoping cover, to prevent loose clothing from getting caught in its high speed rotating shaft.

Leonard noticed this farmer's shield was off—in fact, he didn't even have a place to hook one onto the tractor.

So Leonard climbed off the tractor and put a shield over the ditcher section of the take-off. The farmer tried to stop him. "Don't do that. I don't want one on and I ain't gonna have one."

Leonard started the tractor and saw the exposed whirling shaft and thought, *Whoop, I don't want that.* So he got down again, took the shield and hung it from the seat of the tractor so the shaft was completely covered. The farmer tried to tell him again, "Take that thing off. I don't want it there."

"Now listen," Leonard responded in no uncertain terms, "I'm out here demonstrating this machine and if somebody gets hurt on it because this thing is not on, it's my fault. So it's going to be there."

"Well, as soon as you leave I'm going to take it off," the farmer said stubbornly.

"That's up to you, but as long as I'm here it's going to be on there!"

Two weeks later Leonard heard the report that the farmer had his leg amputated as a result of an accident with the power take-off on his tractor.

∞   ∞   ∞

Leonard always enjoyed showing the ditching machine for special occasions because he could perform in front of a larger crowd. Once, Gary asked him to go to a big agricultural convention in Minnesota called the Corn Husking Festival, where farm machinery of all kinds was demonstrated. Leonard pounded in the stakes at the designated plot, and tied the string to guide the depth of his digging. By the time he was finished, a crowd had gathered.

When he started digging the trench, the crowd was so solid around the machine they kept bumping the string. In addition to his usual routine, Leonard good-naturedly hollered, "Hey, get off my string!" They backed up temporarily and five minutes later would be in the same place. He made a big show about grumbling at them again and said, "Now I hate to be bossy but I can't do a good job if you keep moving that string!" From eleven o'clock in the morning until four o'clock in the afternoon he had a crowd around his machine, there was so much interest in it.

Every time Leonard went out demonstrating or repairing the machines, Vermeer Manufacturing paid him wages. In addition to that, he got royalties on his invention for over twenty years—sometimes more than four thousand dollars a year—which was more than the average annual salary at that time. Vermeer digging machines are still sold today.

Chapter 12

Junkyards and Axles

Vermeer Manufacturing continued to grow. One of Gary Vermeer's business philosophies was the same as one that Leonard used in the sorghum mill—machinery manufactured from heavy-duty reconditioned used parts would not only be cheaper, but would last much longer.

One part that Gary found to be a particularly good buy was the axles he put in his gear boxes. He bought used, heavy-duty axles, reconditioned them, and installed them in new machinery. The axles were heavier than the machinery required, but that way they never wore out. He had been buying used axles from a junkyard in Des Moines when, in 1955, they suddenly decided to double the price on him. That could really eat into bottom line profits so Gary called Leonard and asked him if he could find axles at the price they had been paying. "Well I don't know," Leonard said. "But I can try." He put an ad in the Des Moines paper to get a feel for availability and got a few replies. He picked up those axles.

As Gary started needing more and more axles, Leonard continued to go farther and farther afield to search for them. Eventually he went all over the United States, combining his love of traveling with business. Vermeers paid him wages, expenses, and mileage for the use of his truck.

Leonard never was a man for formal education. This business of buying axles seemed to him the best education in reading and working with people that anybody could get—better than going to high school and college and graduating with a degree. For ten to fifteen years, Leonard furthered his education in dealing with people. With his sense for reading people, he was good at it. If Gary sent someone else to look for axles they would come back with one or two. If he sent Leonard, he would come back with fifty. It seemed God had given him the ability to negotiate well.

The junkyards and salvage yards were usually in the poorest parts of the cities. Once Leonard was in the slum districts near Deerborn Street in South Chicago, one of the poorest sections of the city at that time. He asked at the junkyard office about axles and they said they didn't have any. A young black boy was in the office at the time and overheard their conversation. When Leonard walked out of the office the boy approached him and asked, "Are you the one buyin' axles?"

"Yep," Leonard answered.

"What kind?"

"Well, I have two of them in my pickup." He walked

Junkyards and Axles

over and opened the tailgate. "If they don't look exactly like this I don't want 'em." He made himself perfectly clear.

"That's what I got!" the boy answered enthusiastically.

"Where are they?" Leonard queried.

"I'll show you," the boy answered and climbed in the truck. They drove a few blocks and standing on the corner was another black boy about the same age and build, motioning him to pull over. Leonard was going to ignore him, but the boy sitting next to him said, "That's my buddy." So Leonard pulled over and picked him up.

That's when he got his first scent of danger. Here he was in the worst slum district in Chicago, outnumbered and not knowing where he was going. The first boy directed him about a half mile further underneath the overhead expressway where all the houses were vacant, with broken windows and graffiti written on the walls. The two showed him to a vacant lot, crowded with weeds and other junk, and pointed out a few axles. Leonard saw immediately that they were not what he was looking for and told the boys, "These ain't what I want."

"Now wait a minute, old man," the first one started getting nasty. "You said you wanted axles and here you got some. You'd better take them and pay up." He looked threatening.

Leonard was scared, but tried not to show it. He walked them back to the pickup, opened the gate, pointed inside, looked them straight in the eyes and said firmly once again, "I told you I did not want them if they were not exactly like that."

Surprisingly, the boys backed down and responded, "Okay, just drive us home then."

Leonard knew he needed to confront them before he got to their home ground. He needed to pick the time and place. That was the only way he was going to get out of that dangerous situation without getting himself hurt. He knew if he could get back into a populated area he would have a better chance of getting rid of them. They drove for five minutes and all Leonard saw was more slums. Finally they turned onto a busier thoroughfare and Leonard seized an opportunity.

He saw a parking space along the street and without warning slammed on the brakes, swerved into the parking place, jerked the keys out of the ignition and intimidatingly said, "Get out!" They were so surprised, they just opened the door and got out.

∞   ∞   ∞

Leonard was usually willing to go out looking for axles whenever Gary needed them. But Gary knew that when late summer and fall arrived, Leonard's priority was sorghum, and they couldn't depend on him. In August, 1965, Leonard was making some major improvements to the sorghum mill. He was in the process of welding a huge steel bin, into which the wagons dumped the chopped cane pieces before going through the mill.

Gary called him one day and said, "Leonard, we're desperate for axles. I know you're working on mill improvements, but can you go find some for us?"

Junkyards and Axles

"Well, Gary, I'm making that bin and I sure hate to stop. I'll tell you what I'll do. I'll go, and for every day I'm gone you give me an experienced welder out of your shop to work at my place to help me when I get back." Gary was glad to do that so Leonard started out for Kansas City, Missouri.

Leonard looked through junkyards in towns along the way all day and only found one axle. He thought to himself, *Boy, Gary's gonna come up on the short end of this deal*! It was just about quitting time, but Leonard wasn't quite ready to give up for the day. On the outskirts of the city he came across a junkyard out in the middle of nowhere. They had a number of axles that were still in the frame. He made arrangements for them to be cut out and for the Vermeer truck to pick them up the next day. Since it wasn't quite dark yet, he went on a little further and stayed overnight in a small town. By the end of the next day he not only had his truck loaded, he almost had enough to fill the semitrailer that Vermeer was sending.

∞ ∞ ∞

Just like the digging machine demonstrations, Leonard had a certain method he liked to use when buying axles. It was always his plan to approach a prospect on his own terms, not the other guy's. He found out how many they had, but he never asked how much they wanted for them. He waited until they asked *him* what he was willing to pay. That way he could have the upper hand in the bargaining. But that policy was worth it only if the deal was a big one.

When he used to browse junkyards near Sully to find equipment to use in the sorghum mill, Leonard first asked how much they wanted for something. They named a price higher than they actually expected to get, and the bargaining began. The one who got closest to his original price was the winner.

That didn't work with axles. Typically the junkyards sold the axles for forty-five to seventy-five dollars apiece. Leonard was willing to buy them at thirty to thirty-five dollars apiece, but his starting price was twenty-five. In a typical bargaining session, their prices never met. So unless Leonard got the guy to ask him how much he was willing to pay, or the junkyard owner figured out he needed to name a price in the thirty dollar range instead of the fifty dollar range, the deal wouldn't work. Whichever way it worked, Leonard always stayed in control.

When Leonard went into a junkyard, his methods were not what the owners expected. They couldn't understand how Leonard was trying to do business because he had such a different system. He found out many times that because he was just a little bit different he had the advantage over another. He somehow set people on edge and they didn't know what to expect from him.

Once Leonard was working his way home from Michigan. He was in Toledo, Ohio, and had never been there before. Unknown to him, Harry Vermeer, Gary's brother, had been trying desperately to reach him because they were completely out of axles. Harry had left messages at the places he thought Leonard would stop,

Junkyards and Axles

but had missed him every time.

Leonard turned into the driveway of a large salvage yard on the outskirts of Toledo. He found a gold mine. This salvage yard had axles stacked up like cord wood, just like he was looking for. So Leonard began his plan.

He started out talking to the boss in the office. Leonard was trying to find out three things: why they had so many, what they had paid for them, and what was the prospect of buying them. He wanted the history. The men at the junkyard were trying to find out how badly he wanted them so they could decide how much to charge. Although both parties were constantly thinking price, no one brought it up.

The boss turned Leonard over to the yard foreman who talked to him outside for a half hour. Next he talked to the shop foreman. They kept him jockeying back and forth talking about everything except price. Each man had his own approach.

By talking to the three men separately Leonard was able to piece together the whole situation. The junkyard had been selling the axles to a company in Taiwan and shipping them overseas. Their overseas buyers had quit buying and now the axles were all surplus, which meant they could get ten dollars apiece for them if they were cut up and sold for scrap iron.

Leonard had driven on their yard at twelve noon. At three o'clock he was sitting across the table from the boss and they were deadlocked. Eventually Leonard said in as meek a voice as he could muster, "Look a here, I've been here for three hours and so far all we've argued about is how many you've got and what's the future for them." They both knew they were only worth junk price to the junkyard owner.

Finally the owner said in a coarse voice, "I won't take less than thirty dollars apiece. What are you paying?"

Leonard responded, "Two bits."

The owner hit the table with his hand and let his breath out in an explosive sigh of disgust, "Uhh!" He acted like he had been mightily insulted.

Leonard didn't even argue with him. He got up off his chair, walked to the door and put his hand on the knob. As he was pulling the door open, Leonard asked one more time, "I don't suppose it would hurt to ask you what your best price is." He had asked, but in the circumstances he was still in command of the situation.

The owner repeated himself, "I won't take less than thirty dollars."

Then Leonard pulled the old salesman trick. "I don't care what *I* pay for them. I'd give you a hundred dollars apiece for them. But I've got to satisfy my boss. Let me use your phone and I'll call him. I'll reverse the charges."

That's when the junkyard owner gave the whole game away completely. He said, "On a deal like that, you don't need to reverse the charges."

"That ain't the way we do business," Leonard told him. "I'll reverse the charges." But the guy had given himself away. He had as much as told Leonard that he was anxious to deal. That was the unwritten language Leonard had learned to read.

He called Harry, and Harry was talking so loudly on the phone about how desperate they were for axles, that

Leonard was afraid he would give the whole bluff away. Harry told Leonard to write up a contract for fifty right away at thirty dollars apiece. Leonard knew that thirty dollars was more than acceptable to Vermeers. He had just wanted to see if he could get the junkyard owner any lower. But he could tell the guy was as low as he was going to get.

As they were writing up the contract, Leonard told the boss about the junkyard in Des Moines and how they had suddenly raised the price on them. "Are you going to do the same thing?" he questioned.

"No," he was assured, "As long as we got 'em, the price will be thirty dollars."

Vermeer's bought axles from him by the semitrailer load for years. A few years later the same junkyard owner told Harry he was willing to sell a number of axles and wanted forty-five dollars each. Harry objected and told him he had to think about it. He contacted Leonard. They were needing more and more and had paid forty-five dollars for some already. Harry asked, "What shall we do? They want to charge us forty-five for them."

"Yeah," Leonard answered. "Times is changin'. I suppose that's the best you can do." An hour later he got to thinking about that day, years earlier. *Whoop, I made a deal with that guy,* he thought, *that he would never raise the price.* He called Harry back on the phone and told him.

Harry called the junkyard owner on the phone and said, "Say, I just talked to Leonard and he tells me you made a deal with him that you would never raise the price." They continued to get them for thirty dollars.

∞ ∞ ∞

Leonard learned to recognize valuable junk when he saw a use for it. Years later he was in a junkyard and saw a huge roll of stainless steel screen with a solid band of steel on each end. It was thirty-nine hundred feet long and four feet wide. He saw an immediate use for the screen in the sorghum mill and figured he could sell it to other sorghum producers too. But he didn't want the solid edges. So he bought the whole thing for a few hundred dollars with the condition that he could cut off the steel edges and sell them back to the junkyard! His son-in-law thought he was crazy, but when Leonard began to sell the screen at sorghum producer's meetings for four dollars a square foot, he thought again. The sorghum producers, who normally paid sixteen dollars a square foot for stainless steel screen, thought they were getting a bargain. It was good for both parties! It didn't take long before Leonard's initial investment was paid for and he was once again taking advantage of an opportunity.

Because Leonard visited junkyards and salvage yards for many years, he gradually acquired a large amount of what some people might call "junk". One sunny afternoon in April, 1953, Leonard was cleaning up around the yard on the home place. His piles of junk around the farmyard were getting too tall, so he used his hay rack to load things up and move them around to different locations. As Leonard was standing on the hay

Junkyards and Axles

rack, he was throwing items off of it onto different piles, according to where he wanted to store them.

He grabbed a heavy, solid wooden door and decided it needed to go on the pile farthest from the hay rack. He knew he couldn't throw it that far, so he put it on edge hoping to cartwheel if off the end of the hay rack and get it some distance toward that pile. As he threw the door off the rack, his glove somehow got caught on the door and pulled him off balance. As one edge of the door hit the ground, the full weight of Leonard's body landed on the other edge.

Leonard broke several ribs on his back, although he didn't know it immediately. He stayed home for a few days, but was feeling so tough that he decided to go to the local doctor. The doctor X-rayed his chest cavity, and when the X-ray came back completely black, the doctor assumed something was wrong with his machine. Actually, Leonard's lungs were filled with blood. He checked himself into the Oskaloosa hospital, but wasn't getting any better, although he stayed there almost a whole month. He had a fever all the time and the doctors couldn't get the blood out of his lungs. Finally Leonard got sick of the whole business and checked himself out.

The local druggist's wife was a nurse and she told Leonard's mother, Henrietta, that Leonard should go to another hospital: the Mayo Clinic in Rochester, Minnesota. Leonard made an appointment and was soon relieved to find that the doctors there knew what to do. In order to drain his lungs, they surgically removed five inches from two of Leonard's ribs, just below his left shoulder blade. The hole was large enough so that the wound could drain and heal properly, from the inside out.

Leonard was released from the hospital in July, but still needed to be nursed at home. He had a gaping hole in his back, two inches by five inches, by one inch deep, that could not get infected. Every day for three months Gertrude sterilized the wound by pouring a hot liquid into it. Leonard complained and complained, not only because he was terribly sore, but also because the liquid was either too hot or too cold! Gertrude never seemed to get it exactly right.

Lawrence, who had quit school the year earlier, managed the sorghum planting and cultivating for the spring and summer. The rest of their ground was rented out. By the time sorghum making season came around, Leonard was getting around well. He lived with that huge hole in his back the rest of his life.

∞   ∞   ∞

Another time, while he was working for Vermeer's during the 1960's, Leonard was at a junkyard in Chicago and asked the owner if they had any axles. "Yeah," the man said. "I need to have fifty dollars apiece for them."

Leonard just gave him his card and said, "We're paying twenty-five. If you get hungry let us know." Then he walked away.

"Hey, wait a minute!"

Leonard knew he would do that and turned around. The junkyard owner was willing to deal.

Junkyards and Axles

Figure 12.1: The Leonard Maasdam family at 25 years, Christmas 1959.

The axles were supposed to be ready to pick up on a certain day. But Leonard had figured out this guy. He was not very reliable. The truck arrived at three o'clock and none of them were ready yet and they were nearly ready to close. Since they were in south Chicago, Leonard asked him, "Where would be a safe place to rent a motel room around here?"

"There's a place five to six blocks away. I'm ready to leave. I could just lead you there." They drove through neighborhoods that didn't look too safe to Leonard, and the farther they went, the worse they looked. Finally the man pointed out the motel and with a wave, disappeared into traffic. Well, now Leonard didn't know where to park the truck. He didn't want to leave it on the street for fear it would be gone by morning. He noticed a police station down the street so decided to park it there.

He walked to a nearby restaurant and found something to eat. But he just didn't feel comfortable. He walked back to the motel and looked into the gaming room where they were playing pool. He didn't like the looks of it either. When he finally went to his room for the night he put a chair in front of the door figuring, at least this way they will have to wake me up if they break in. That was how bad his feeling of danger was.

The next day he returned to the junkyard and the owner asked him, "Did you stay at that motel? Did you see the big guy behind the desk? Do you know who that was?"

"*How would I know?*" Leonard thought.

"That was Al Capone's brother!"

No wonder he had felt that that wasn't a very safe place! But on second thought, maybe it wasn't too bad. The mafia wouldn't want to rob somebody or do damage if it was their own relative's place, right?

∞ ∞ ∞

As Leonard continued to look for axles, he gradually developed a network of junkyards and salvage yards that shipped them to Vermeer's on a regular basis. Once when Leonard was at a junkyard, he came across a little newspaper that circulated exclusively to junkyards in Iowa and the neighboring states. For ten dollars he could put in an ad that went to all the junkyards in that region. Between placing an ad in this paper and developing relationships with junkyards across the country, Leonard eventually worked himself out of a job.

Chapter 13
Water and Wells

On his trips across the country Leonard saw many things that sparked his interest. While looking for axles he had been to California many times and had seen irrigation systems watering the fields. He was fascinated by them because nobody had anything like that in Iowa.

On Monday, July 1, 1956, he and Lawrence, who at age nineteen was tall and broad like his father, were working on the silo. The weather was hot and dry just like it had been all year. Leonard had been thinking about irrigation all morning and abruptly told Lawrence, "I'm going to Newton to find a county agent to get some information on irrigation." He wanted to learn the business.

He quit working and drove to Newton. At the county agent's office he got disgusted. The agent was just like all those educated guys. He didn't know anything about irrigation. He suggested Leonard go to Ames and visit the agricultural college. Maybe they would know more.

Well, Leonard had had a bad experience with the professors at Iowa State University once when he was trying to figure something out for the sorghum mill. He wasn't about to go to them again.

He decided to try Des Moines instead. He found one implement dealer that had literature on irrigation. They had nothing in stock, but were willing to order equipment. Leonard thought their price of $450 for a twenty-five to thirty horse power pump was too much money, so he walked out.

He drove to Gary Vermeer's house in Pella early that evening because he was quite sure Gary had a few extra twenty-five horse power Wisconsin engines that he didn't have any use for. About eight o'clock that night he knocked on Gary's door and when Gary let him in, Leonard asked without preamble, "Say, Gary, do you have any more of them twenty-five horse power engines? I want one to try out irrigation."

Gary had also been interested in irrigation and said, "Well, Leonard, tomorrow morning I've got a truck going to Grand Island, Nebraska to pick up two systems. One for me and one for my neighbor. If you're interested in one, ride along and buy it and you can get it trucked for free!"

Getting something for nothing always appealed to the frugal Dutch side of Leonard's nature, so he asked, "What time are you leaving?"

"At two in the morning from the factory!"

It was eight o'clock at night and he still had to drive the twenty miles back to Sully. But he was back in Pella six hours later. They drove all the way out to Nebraska

Water and Wells

and when they got there it was horribly hot—a hundred and eight degrees in the shade and there was no shade available. All the work they had to do to get the pipes ready was outside, and it was so hot and dry that everyone was miserable. Finally they got three complete irrigation systems—pipe, sprinklers, and pump—loaded on the truck.

The day after they got back, Leonard learned his first lesson in irrigation—sprinkle the water on slowly. They were very eager to get the engine pumping, but it was a lot of work to lay out all the pipe with the sprinklers, and then they had chores to do too. So, to see how it would work, Leonard just put a section of pipe in the river, started the pump for five minutes and let the water run all over the corn field. A large area was flooded in a short amount of time.

The next morning, when they got back outside, they laid the rest of the pipe and attached the sprinklers. When they got to the area they had flooded, it was all nice and green so they decided not to put any sprinkler heads there. They set the sprinklers to put on water at the rate of a half inch per hour for four hours, and then moved the pipes to the next field.

A week later Leonard went back to his first field and saw that the corn in the flooded area that had looked so good, was actually withered and dying. The water had packed the ground, then dried it into a hard crust which cracked open. The rest of the field was luscious and green. He had read in the instruction book about putting water on slowly, but now he experienced the results of flood irrigation himself. Like so many other things in life, the experience taught him well.

The irrigation system that Leonard had purchased consisted of a forty foot long pipe that was four inches in diameter. It lay on the ground between the rows of crop. A long riser pipe with a sprinkler head on top rose above the crop at regular intervals. The biggest drawback to the system was that after irrigating, the pipes had to be picked up by hand and moved over thirty rows to the next area that needed irrigation. When irrigating corn or cane the pipes had to be held way over head because the crop was so tall. That was hard work.

Leonard had Lawrence, Darlene and Marjorie helping him move the pipes. They grumbled and complained, but didn't have a choice whether or not they wanted to help. The girls especially hated it when the corn was so high that they had to hold the pipes over their heads. The dirty water ran down their arms and made a mess. They went barefoot because the fields were muddy and feet were much easier to clean than shoes.

Once, when it was particularly dry, they even had to get up during the night to move the irrigation pipes. That night Lawrence told Leonard, "Dad, this is too hard of work. You've got to be able to come up with something better than this." Leonard got to thinking that he agreed with him. But he hadn't come up with any ideas for improving it, yet.

Even though 1956 was a very dry year, the Maasdam's harvest was an excellent one. They were the only farmers around that used irrigation and since everyone wanted water, their system drew a lot of attention. Peo-

Water and Wells

ple came from all over to look at it.

After harvest, Leonard approached Gary Vermeer and suggested that maybe they sell irrigation equipment. At first he wasn't too interested, but finally agreed when Leonard said he would do the actual selling. The following January found Leonard visiting all the people who had been to see his irrigation site. He visited more to talk than to sell. In fact, one customer told him later that he sounded more like he was trying to convince him *not* to buy an irrigation system. Having a system was hard work, and Leonard didn't want to mislead anyone. By March, however, he had sold his first system for Pella Irrigation Company, as he, Gary and Ralph Vermeer named their latest venture.

Leonard had it in his mind all along to make something mechanical so those pipes wouldn't have to be moved by hand. An engineer at Vermeers, Arnold Mathes, who was also Leonard's cousin (the inventive genius ran in the family), had designed a high clearance machine that straddled the corn. The farmer laid the pipes directly on the irrigation equipment to carry them in and out of the field. But neither Arnold nor Gary were very happy with how it worked.

One day Leonard, Gertrude and her sister Johanna were on their way home from a shopping trip to Des Moines. Leonard had had this irrigation business in the back of his mind all day long and suddenly he got an idea. Johanna must have seen the look on his face because she said, "Len, what are you thinking about?"

"I just had a crazy idea," he answered. Before he got home he had the whole machine planned in his mind.

The next day he went over to Gary's and talked with him and Arnold. He told them his idea and drew out sketches of it with chalk on the cement floor. Arnold looked down at what he had drawn and said, "That's it! That's your answer!"

Vermeers built the sprinkler system like he said. They built a tower on a four wheel wagon that had long aluminum sprinkler pipes sticking out perpendicular on each side, with guide wires to brace them. They put a nozzle on each end, and another nozzle every twenty feet, all the way to the center. The nozzles got gradually smaller towards the center of the sprinkler. Each one was turned the same direction, except one to provide back pressure, so the whole top revolved. The machine watered a three hundred foot circle. They used cable on a tractor to pull the machine from one station to another.

The first time Leonard and Gary tried out the machine they had far too much pressure coming in and not enough bracing. The whole thing was too flimsy and fell apart. They were not discouraged at all. On the contrary, they were very enthused! They worked on it some more and fixed it so that instead of being flat out from the center tower, the pipes were pointed up a bit. They also made the pipes out of steel and braced the whole thing more thoroughly. That was it. It worked! The pipes went around and around and gave the whole area a nice, even sprinkle.

Vermeers named it the 140 because it was one hundred forty feet long. They sold them all over the United States and Canada. They even shipped some to South

Figure 13.1: Leonard's irrigation system, circa 1957.

America to water banana trees—only the tower had to be taller than the seventeen foot banana trees they were watering!

Leonard's design worked fine as long as the ground to be irrigated was near a river. More often than not, though, that was not the case. In order to have a good water flow through the system, the pipes needed a well that could pump water five hundred to a thousand gallons per minute. No drilling rigs in Iowa could dig that type of a well.

So Gary had Leonard and Arnold go to see a drilling rig in Grand Island, Nebraska, to find out if it was something they could build. It was quite complicated so they decided to buy one instead. The rig was capable of digging a thirty-eight inch diameter hole.

For four or five years Leonard dug wells all over the area with Vermeers' drilling rig. He dug about fifty wells during that period of time, and, by experience soon came to learn where to expect to find water and where not.

Since Leonard charged twenty-five dollars for every foot he sunk the well, farmers generally tried to get him to dig on low ground. But Leonard had learned through observation and experience that low ground was generally not where he would find the greatest capacity wells. The farmers were not always ready to agree with him. Once when Leonard wanted to dig in a different spot, the farmer told him, "If the test hole you drill is better than mine I'll pay for the test, but if it's not you pay for it." Sure enough, Leonard's was quite a bit better.

Arie Lanser's new farm had a shallow creek bottom

Water and Wells

on it with fine sand. He had a farm well dug there, but it was always giving him trouble. There was lots of water only fifteen feet deep, but the sand kept getting in the well and ruining the pump. Leonard put in a deeper well for him and managed to keep the sand from getting in the pump.

∞   ∞   ∞

Once he was down in Illinois in the Mississippi River bottom. This farmer had a square farm and he wanted the well dug in the middle so his pipe could go in all directions. Leonard only charged a dollar per foot for test drilling, so gave it a try even though he didn't think they would find water there. It was low capacity. Leonard suggested trying higher ground. But the farmer wanted his well closer to the house and the road. They ran another test drill and it was low too. The farmer couldn't understand it. His neighbor had a well at that level and it was fine. Finally the farmer allowed Leonard to drill where he wanted. He went to a little higher ground and dug ninety-four feet down. His well produced two to three thousand gallons of water per minute! They could never figure out why he was always right. Leonard himself didn't really know. He just had a feel for things that must have been God-given.

He had flown over the Mississippi River many times and observed the nature of the water flow and the terrain of the land. He saw that at one time the river bottom had been much lower than at present. As sediment continued to flow down the river it filled in the bottom.

From his experience, wells dug slightly above the Mississippi River valley were more likely to have water in them than those in the bottom of it. He didn't exactly know why, but time and again, his theory proved true. At different times Leonard would dig up driftwood, shells and fish fragments from sixty to eighty feet below the ground.

∞ ∞ ∞

Soon after Pella Irrigation Company was founded, Gary suggested that the company buy an airplane to make customer visits in less time. Leonard spoke up right away, "If Pella Irrigation is gonna buy a plane, I'm gonna learn to fly it!" That was exactly what Gary wanted him to say.

One of Gary's workers in the plant knew how to fly airplanes so Gary gave him time off and paid his fees to teach Leonard how to fly. That way they could avoid the high-priced instructors in Des Moines.

Leonard learned to fly and then earned his instrument rating too. His instructor covered the windshield with paper and Leonard had to fly without seeing anything. At one point he felt like the airplane was going down. He pulled back on the stick and it was solid. It wouldn't come back. He hollered to his instructor in the back seat, "Let go of that stick!"

"I'm not holding on to it!" came the reply. "Now fly the plane!"

They were in a death spiral and the harder Leonard pulled back on the stick, the tighter spiral he went into.

Figure 13.2: Leonard and Gertrude, March 1965. Leonard flew them to North Dakota to visit Darlene and her husband Paul Schoon.

Since he had been flying blind he had become disoriented. As soon as he realized what was happening he worked the opposite rudder with his feet and pulled out of the spiral.

Leonard enjoyed flying and digging those wells. He found the geology of the different types of soil extremely interesting. He thought that if he had known about geology as a boy he would have wanted to have schooling in it.

He dug wells for several years. Eventually that area of the country began having more seasonal rains again, and farmers realized that irrigation in Iowa was not really necessary. It always rained just before it was too late. An investment in an irrigation system was worth it maybe once in twenty years.

Leonard collected royalties for his irrigation sprinkler design for ten years. After that the modern design for sprinklers came into use—one with a central hub and a long pipe with wheels attached to it that traveled in a big circle. At first that machine caused trouble because each of the wheels on the circle had to travel at different speeds. As that machine improved and Leonard's did not, his became obsolete.

Pella Irrigation Company was still in operation, but about 1960, since irrigation was in a decline in Iowa, the company began to change it's emphasis. Gary had been looking for an opportunity to sell his farming equipment factory direct, without hurting the dealers he had already acquired. So he hired Carl Boat as a manager and one-fourth owner to expand Pella Irrigation Company's operations. Later George Wassenaar also joined the company.

Both men knew how to do their jobs and the company grew and grew. In 1982 Leonard and Harry Vermeer decided to sell their quarter interests in Pella Irrigation. Leonard walked away with a check for a third of a million dollars—having put nothing into the company but his time and a few good ideas.

Chapter 14

Two Round Houses

Leonard lived in the house that he built just down from the home place for sixteen years, but eventually Gertrude wanted to move to Pella. They moved in 1957, the year their son Lawrence got married. They lived in Pella, at 511 Main Street, for a number of years, but Leonard never really liked living in town. In 1972 he started looking for an acreage in the countryside outside of Pella where he could build a house, but couldn't find anything.

Finally he found a choice spot three miles north of Pella, but the stubborn farmer wouldn't sell just a few acres! He had fifty-two acres in that spot that were all hills, gullies and timber, and he wanted to sell it all or nothing.

Leonard looked it all over and got to thinking. *He had spent a long time looking for a place in the country and this was the only spot anywhere around.* He reasoned that if he wanted it, others would too. He decided there was probably a market for development lots and he intended to capitalize on it.

"Now listen," Leonard started in on the farmer, "I'll never be able to farm this ground. It's too hilly. How much are you selling it for?"

Leonard knew exactly what answer the farmer would give and he was not disappointed. "How much will you give?" the farmer asked.

"I'll give you top farm price," Leonard answered. At that time top farm price was close to five hundred dollars an acre.

So Leonard got his ground and at age sixty-seven started to build his house. But he didn't want to build just any house. Contrary as ever, he wanted something different. He had been told that it was impossible to build a round house with a dome roof and have decently shaped rooms, so that is what he decided to try. He built a round house, as he liked to say with a twinkle in his eye, "so his wife could never catch him in a corner."

The rooms in the house were vaguely wedge-shaped, like pieces of a pie. The kitchen and the living room took up one half of the structure, and a bedroom, bath, utility and sewing room filled the rear half. Half of the house contained a second level with two more bedrooms and a bath. The garage and breezeway extended off to one side.

The main circular section of the house was forty feet across and the top of the dome, which has no interior supports, towered twenty-two feet above the floor. Leonard built a circular staircase all the way to the top of the dome where he situated a clear plastic lookout

Figure 14.1: Leonard's first round house, 1973.

bubble.

Of course he used salvaged materials throughout the fifteen month construction process. For the walls of the basement, he had masons lay big hollow clay tile that he had retrieved out of a brick kiln that went out of business. He got the brick for the outer walls from the same place.

Leonard, loving gadgets like he does, filled the house with grown-up toys to entertain visitors. He built a 120 foot train track around the perimeter of the house at the base of the dome. The flatbed train cars carried trinkets from their travels, and more toys, such as miniature steam engines, a stage coach, and a replica of a Jackson touring car his grandfather used to drive. Each car's load was seen as the train circled the living room. Then it went through a hole in the wall, climbed to a bedroom on the second level, continued through the second upstairs room, and back down into the living room.

To light the living room, Leonard wired a huge wagon wheel with lights and motorized it so that it turned. He acquired chandelier crystals from somewhere and attached them to the wheel so they shimmered in the light as they moved. Finally, he bought a glass covered ball used in the discotheques of that era, and hung it on the cable supporting the wheel so that when the wheel turned, it turned too. The effect was magnificent.

He also had an artist paint a mural using "invisible" paints on one section of the ceiling. The scene depicted the stable where Jesus was born, complete with shepherds and angels. During the day the mural looked like dark smudges on the ceiling, but when the lights were out and the black light bulbs on, the painting showed up beautifully.

Later, when Leonard wanted a few more toys for his new house, he bought a fifty-year-old, four-thousand piece elephant collection from a woman in Minnesota for twenty-five thousand dollars. The collection came with sixty antique showcases that he put throughout the house to display elephants of all shapes, sizes, and materials.

He loved to give tours of his house (and still does!), which had hardly changed since he and Gertrude built it. While visitors were there he probably treated them to a few of his favorite practical jokes. One that worked almost every time, Leonard said, was to put a glass of water under a hat and claim he could drink the water without touching the hat. Then he made motions over the hat and said this or that and declared, "Well, take a look." The unsuspecting guest lifted the hat and Leonard picked up the glass and drank the water!

He had another favorite he liked to play on "educated" people. He said, "Now you know figures don't lie and bankers honor and all that; well, listen to this. I put fifty dollars in the bank. I write a check for twenty and that leaves thirty. I write another check for fifteen dollars and that leaves fifteen in there. I write a check for nine dollars leaving six and finally write one last check for six dollars leaving zero. The next day I get a notice from the bank saying I'm a dollar overdrawn so I go to the bank with a chip on my shoulder and really tell them they made a mistake. They say, 'wait a minute, don't be so fast. This adds up to fifty-one dollars and you're overdrawn.' Are you one of them real smart ones? I'll let you think through that."

$$\begin{array}{cc} & \$50 \\ \$20 & \$30 \\ 15 & 15 \\ 9 & 6 \\ \underline{6} & \underline{0} \\ 50 & 51 \end{array}$$

Just as Leonard expected, it wasn't long before people started to come to him wanting to buy a few acres on which to build a house. He began to sell parcels ranging in size from five to ten acres for thirteen hundred to four thousand dollars per acre! Considering they would pay the same price for a small lot in Pella, the people were happy to pay that price. It was just one more opportunity of which Leonard took advantage.

Leonard worked hard at making the development a desirable place to live. He planted several areas with thousands of walnut trees and kept them nicely pruned so one day they could be harvested for lumber. For a seventy year old man to plant a grove of slow-growing walnut trees is to be optimistic about the future. He also put in a road through the property for accessibility and drilled wells for water. He even offered to finance the home construction of the people who bought ground from him.

∞ ∞ ∞

One Sunday evening Leonard was over at the neighbors talking. The sky had been getting darker and darker and the wind had picked up considerably. They suddenly noticed a funnel cloud out in the west and decided to get inside. The tornado struck the neighbor's house, tearing off part of the roof. Leonard was left wondering what happened to his house.

He went home and found a little damage. The garage had been damaged pretty badly and the pressure from outside had caused the bubble at the top of the dome to blow off. If he hadn't had the bubble, the roof would have sustained considerably more damage. Leonard patched the hole with plywood and bolted it to the roof securely.

One week later, the sky was dark and threatening again. Leonard was looking outside when he saw a tornado coming from the west. He had just decided to join Gertrude in the basement. What he didn't see was the tornado already upon him coming from the southwest. Before he went downstairs, Leonard wanted to step out on the porch one more time to sense the atmosphere in the air.

He tried to push the latch on the screen door, but it wouldn't open! Momentarily he thought it was locked, but then again, knew it wasn't. He thought, *maybe I better not go out.* Just at that moment he felt such strong pressure from behind him that the latch broke. He heard it snap and at the same time heard the window blow out behind him and felt a strong push on his back. Whoooosh! He had been moved ten feet and was standing outside! He didn't know what had happened, but one second he was inside looking out, and the next he was outside. They never found a sliver of broken glass and Leonard was shaken, but unhurt.

He had heard of people who sat by airplane doors and had gotten sucked out. He had always thought, *why don't they hang on?* Now he understood. There was absolutely no chance to do anything in circumstances like that. Except for a few broken windows, and a missing plywood "dome", Leonard's round house was basically undamaged.

∞ ∞ ∞

In 1980, when the energy crisis was in full swing, Leonard (age 76) decided to build another round house. This one was earth-sheltered and just down the hill. He had his grandsons help him build it in about two years.

Unlike the first house, the second one did not have wooden rafters. Leonard made forms and poured concrete, six sections at a time, three different times. He had long support poles under each section until the concrete hardened. When the poles loosened Leonard knew the cement had hardened enough and went on with the next section. The interior dome of the roof was finished with small wood pieces, shaped slightly wider at the bottom than at the top, so the entire domed ceiling was covered.

On his trip to Japan, Leonard had seen a lot of interesting Oriental architecture. He decided to include some in this house. He built a structure similar to a pagoda over the kitchen table, complete with a roof that curved upward at each corner. He built another one over the island in the kitchen.

Since most of the house was buried in the ground, Leonard wanted to be sure that each room had some natural light, so he made indoor windows at the tops of the walls for the back bedrooms. Like the first house, this one had a circular staircase climbing all the way to the top of the dome. Once at the top, though, the scenery was ground level.

When the house was finished Leonard and Gertrude lived there until 1991, but Leonard never liked it as well as his first round house.

Chapter 15

Sorghum Producers Organize

When he wasn't building houses, making deals or making sorghum, Leonard always found something to do. For instance, when Jimmy Carter was elected president in 1976, Leonard took a liking to him. He thought Carter seemed like a decent Christian man so he decided to attend his inauguration the following January.

A Des Moines man had chartered a bus and Leonard caught it in Ottumwa. They traveled the whole night and enjoyed a few days of sight-seeing before the ceremonies. On the day of the inauguration, Leonard got to the mall early. There was standing room only waiting outside the gates to get into the mall. People packed the area and he had to wait forty-five minutes before they opened the gate.

Leonard appreciated President Carter's inaugural address, especially when he asked God Almighty to help him in his endeavor. He seemed like a good man.

After the address, Leonard joined the crowds thronging on Pennsylvania Avenue, hoping for a glimpse of the president and his family in their motorcade. Just before the motorcade got to where Leonard was standing, President Jimmy Carter and his family got out of the car and began to walk! They were only ten feet away and Leonard was thrilled! The secret service agents around the president, and on top of the surrounding buildings, were not so thrilled, but Carter was a man of the people, and with the people he would be.

A few years later Leonard was down in Plains, Georgia and saw the president's former home. He also attended a reception for Billy Carter.

In his travels down south he had been noticing that many of the sorghum jars he found in the stores did not contain pure sorghum. They were often a blend of a little sorghum, molasses, corn syrup, and sugar water—ingredients that were much cheaper to use.

Leonard and the other sorghum producers in the country were concerned because the mislabeled syrup provided illegal competition to their product. Because it contained inferior ingredients the producers could sell it at a lower price. In addition, if people bought a jar labeled sorghum that contained mostly blackstrap molasses, it tasted much more bitter than the real thing. Customers would think, "Well if that's what sorghum tastes like, I don't want any."

In response Leonard took several courses of action. In January, 1983, he began writing a monthly newsletter

Sorghum Producers Organize

called the "The Sweet Sorghum Press." He published it for several years and sent it to dozens of sorghum producers across the southeast. As he developed his mailing list, Leonard began to realize that there was an interest in a national association. Sorghum making was a cottage industry with no guidelines or way to disseminate information. The sorghum producers needed an organization.

An extension agent named Ivon McCarty had organized a local educational meeting on sorghum production in Manchester, Tennessee, expecting twelve to fifteen people to show up. Leonard somehow heard about the meeting and wrote about it in his newsletter. Sixty-seven people showed up for the gathering—most of them from out of state! That was the first unofficial meeting of the Sweet Sorghum Growers Association.

The growers met for three years and each year interest in forming an official organization grew. Finally in March, 1986 the National Sweet Sorghum Producers and Processors Association (NSSPPA) was chartered. Most of the names of sorghum grower contacts came from Leonard's "Sweet Sorghum Press" mailing list. Currently the NSSPPA meetings occur on an annual basis and have about 250 people in attendance from twenty-three states and Mexico.

One of the first projects the newly formed association took on was the development of a sweet sorghum logo which appeared only on jars of pure sorghum. Blended products were not allowed to use the label.

At the same time, Leonard began to work with the Iowa Department of Agriculture and the U.S. Food and

Drug Administration. After repeated trips to Des Moines and even a trip to Washington D.C., their agents collected samples of the suspected mislabeled sorghum and sent it to a laboratory where a chemical method for distinguishing true sorghum from its imitators had been developed.

Thousands of cases of mislabeled sorghum were embargoed, but the struggle continued. Producers received large fines and had their mislabeled product confiscated, but a short time later they were back doing the same thing. Sorghum, it seemed, wasn't of enough importance in the market to warrant the regulation necessary to keep it pure. At age 90 Leonard is still fighting the same battle.

∞ ∞ ∞

As Leonard grew older he gradually began to slow down. He still delivered sorghum because he could drive well, but he let his son-in-law Charles handle more and more of the operation of the sorghum mill. Gertrude began to slow down too, although she was still involved in her Circle group at church.

In his younger years, Leonard was out to make as much money as he could. But as he grew older and he and Gertrude began to realize how much they had, he thought they should do something special with it. They agreed to buy a farm and set it up so all the net proceeds went to charity. When they first started looking, there were no farms for sale, but within a few months something opened up and Leonard bought it.

Sorghum Producers Organize

Figure 15.1: Fiftieth wedding anniversary, January 24, 1984.

The day they signed the final papers making the arrangements for the charity farm at the lawyers office, Leonard and Gertrude went out for coffee to celebrate. Later that day Leonard brought Gertrude to Pella for her Circle meeting in the afternoon since she didn't drive anymore.

Leonard drove to church to pick her up later and found her just putting her shoes on. She started a letter to her grandson Larry that evening, planning to finish it the next day, the day before their fifty-seventh wedding anniversary.

In the morning, Leonard usually got up before Gertrude and read the paper. When she wasn't up by the time he finished it, he went in to wake her. Putting his hand on her shoulder he felt it immediately. She was cold. During the night she had made a sound, a gurgling he couldn't quite describe. He was going to get up and turn the lights on, but decided that since it was often hard for her to get to sleep again, he wouldn't wake her. *I want her to sleep*, he thought.

That sound was her last breath. Leonard called his daughter, Marjorie, first, and asked her to tell the others. He let his daughters make all the arrangements for the funeral, characteristically telling them, "Don't get the highest price casket nor the cheapest, just get something good that will look nice."

The morning of the funeral, Leonard was up extremely early. He sat in his favorite chair in their sitting area and in his shaky handwriting and with his eighth grade education, wrote his wife a letter.

> 5:o clock, Jan 26 - 1991
>
> To my dear beuloved wife
>
> I thank God for trusted help mate through out my jurney through life and the wonderfull way God took you home and my prayer is that on the apponted time he will take me home the same way. Someday we will meet again.
>
> Oh Lord, give me strent wile hear on earth to do your purpose.
>
> I am writing assurded that God will lead me on what journey there is left here on earth and can meet you in Glory.
>
> The clock just strock 6. One hour closer.
>
> By By for now
>
> L.J.M.

Later that day, after the funeral but before they took the casket to the cemetery, Leonard asked for a few minutes alone with Gertrude. He took the letter he had written to her and put it in her hand. He said later that he had written it so he could continue on, so he would live up to the promises he had made to her.

In the months after his wife's funeral, Leonard slowly adjusted to living his life without his lifelong mate. He learned to cook a few things, moved into the upper round house (the one he liked best), and continued to make sorghum, being just as demanding and ornery as ever around the crew. Every year he says he gets slower and weaker, but he's still very much alive and celebrated his ninety-first birthday on November 18, 1995.

Leonard once compared his life to King Solomon's in the Bible. Solomon asked for wisdom and God gave him riches and long life too. All Leonard asked for was a Christian home blessed with children, and God blessed him with everything else. How long he'll live he doesn't know but he wants to be faithful with the resources and the time he has left.

Index

Accidents, 4, 68, 75, 120, 133
Airplanes, 26, 108, 148, 160

Boat, Carl, 150
Breeding horses, 20
Buying axles, 123

California, 94, 96, 139
Carter, President Jimmy, 163
Charitable activities, 94, 166
Chicago World's Fair, 59
Corn syrup, 3, 164

Deafness, 6, 7, 96, 100
Deal, making a, 40, 108, 127, 132, 143
Different approach, 6, 7, 128
Drilling wells, 146, 158
Dutch, 4, 19, 30, 58, 63, 74, 93, 140

Dynamite, 8, 10, 11

Education, philosophy of, 3, 18, 25, 67, 68, 78, 84, 124, 142, 146
Elephant collection, 157

Farm ground, purchase of, 40, 41, 95, 154, 166
Financial goals, 8, 27, 29, 67
Foot accident, 20, 37
Fourth of July, 8, 26, 30, 42

Geology, 148, 150
Great Depression, 17, 20, 28, 31, 33, 39

Helping others get started, 54, 62, 88, 94
Hired help, 45, 48, 49, 50, 55, 59, 65

philosophy of, 43
House construction, 95, 154, 160

Inflammatory rheumatism, 15, 27
Irrigation, 139, 150

Jacobsen, Lola, 25, 27
Jokes and pranks, 33, 35, 56, 96, 157

Kramer
    Charles, 88, 90, 166
    John, 76
    Marjorie, 65, 66, 67, 68, 88, 142, 168

Lanser, Arie, 54, 146
Louisiana, 76, 83, 84
Lynnville, Iowa, 41, 54, 101

Maasdam
    Darlene, 65, 66, 67, 142
    Fred, 16, 37, 38, 39, 40, 74, 79, 81, 88
    Harlan, 88
    Henrietta, 1, 3, 42, 45, 52
    Henry, 10, 26, 27, 38

Lane, 2, 3, 8, 10, 13, 14, 17, 20, 21, 22, 37, 48, 64, 74, 79, 81
Lawrence, 63, 64, 66, 68, 134, 139, 142, 153
Marie, 15, 16, 26, 38, 43, 45, 58
Mafia, 137
Mathes
    Arnold, 143
    Grandpa, 31, 35, 40, 62
McCarty, Ivon, 165
Measles, 1, 13, 14, 25
Mechanical ability, 14, 53, 83, 84, 86, 105, 143
Molasses, 164

Opportunity, recognition of, 20, 35, 107, 126, 132, 139, 154

Pella, Iowa, 5, 28, 30, 34, 68, 77, 87, 88, 102, 109, 153
Pella Irrigation Company, 143, 150
People sense, 7, 18, 19, 22, 51, 62, 64, 113,

INDEX

117, 124, 125, 130, 134
Prepared ahead of time, 23, 30, 42, 50, 111

Radio, 7, 96
Religious convictions, 16, 27, 28, 66, 69, 72, 147, 170
Retirement from farming, 93, 94

Salvaging, 7, 17, 74, 77, 78, 79, 86, 87, 89, 90, 91, 105, 132, 156
Selling sorghum, 19, 22
Shivaree, 33
Shooting bolts, 10
Showmanship, 8, 96, 109, 110
Sibling rivalry, 37
Silver bars, 94
Sorghum growers association, 165
Sorghum, part of whole life, 3, 14, 16, 18, 74, 126
Stainless steel, 132
Statue of Opportunity, 7
Stock market, 39
Stuttering, 6

Sully, Iowa, 5, 20, 31, 41, 107, 128, 140
Sweet Sorghum Press newsletter, 165

Telephone, 29
Thriftiness, 7, 26, 29, 33, 55, 59, 63, 75, 76, 79, 86, 95, 123, 140
Tornado, 71, 74, 159

Van Wyk
   Henry, 1, 14, 79, 81
   Wilma, 40
Vermeer
   Gary, 108, 123, 126, 140, 143
   Harry, 128, 130, 151
   Ralph, 109, 143
Vermeer Manufacturing, 109, 118, 121, 123, 131
Verwers, Ben, 62

Wassenaar, George, 150
Wielard
   Gertrude, 28
   Johanna, 31, 45, 54
Work, attitude toward, 13, 38, 67, 93, 142
World War II, 76, 84